Arizona's
Historic
Escapes

Calumet &
Arizona Guest House, Bisbee

ALSO BY KAREN SURINA MULFORD

Arizona's Historic Restaurants and Their Recipes
South Carolina's Historic Restaurants and Their Recipes (with Dawn O'Brien)

Copper Bell Bed-and-Breakfast, Tucson

El Tovar Hotel, Grand Canyon

JOHN F. BLAIR, PUBLISHER
WINSTON-SALEM, NORTH CAROLINA

Arizona's

*The Surgeon's House
Bed-and-Breakfast,
Jerome*

Historic

*Victorian Inn
of Prescott*

Escapes

by
Karen Surina Mulford

The paper in this book meets the
guidelines for permanence and durability
of the Committee on Production Guidelines for Book Longevity
of the Council on Library Resources

DESIGN BY DEBRA LONG HAMPTON
COVER DESIGN BY LIZA LANGRALL
PRINTED AND BOUND BY R. R. DONNELLEY & SONS

Library of Congress Cataloging-in-Publication Data
Mulford, Karen.
    Arizona's historic escapes / by Karen Surina Mulford.
        p.   cm.
    Includes index.
    ISBN 0-89587-202-1 (alk. paper)
    1. Arizona—Guidebooks.   2. Historic sites—Arizona—Guidebooks.
3. Hotels—Arizona—Directories.   I. Title.
F809.3.M85   1997
917.9104'53—dc21   97-33225

For my aunt,
Delores Cobb,
my original travel guide
to the wonders of Arizona

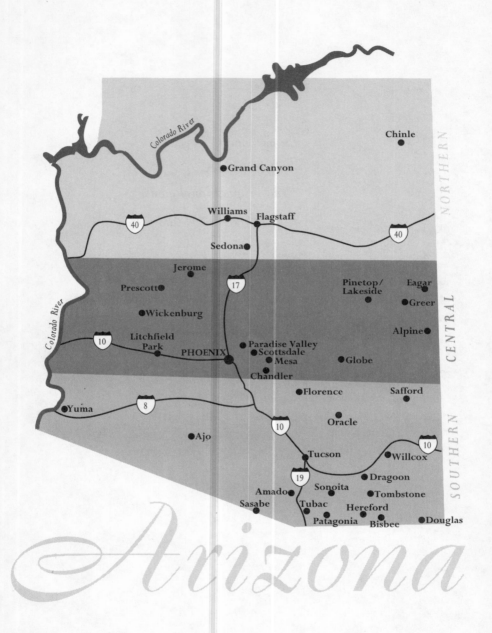

Colorado River

Chinle

Grand Canyon

NORTHERN

Williams Flagstaff

40 40

Sedona

Jerome

Colorado River

Prescott

Pinetop/
Lakeside

Eagar
Greer

17

Wickenburg

Alpine

CENTRAL

Litchfield
Park

10

Paradise Valley
Scottsdale
PHOENIX Mesa
Chandler

Globe

Yuma

8

Florence

Safford

10

Oracle

Ajo

Willcox

10

Tucson

Dragoon

19

Sonoita
Amado

Tombstone

Sasabe Tubac

Hereford

SOUTHERN

Patagonia Bisbee

Douglas

Arizona

Contents

Acknowledgments
Introduction

NORTHERN ARIZONA

Grand Canyon
Bright Angel Lodge   7
El Tovar Hotel   9

Chinle
Thunderbird Lodge   12

Williams
The Johnstonian Bed-and-Breakfast   15
Red Garter Bed-and-Bakery   17

Flagstaff
Birch Tree Inn   19
Dierker House Bed-and-Breakfast   21
Hotel Monte Vista   23
Inn at 410 Bed-and-Breakfast   26

Sedona
Briar Patch Inn   28
Forest Houses   31
Garland's Oak Creek Lodge   33
Lomacasi Cottages Bed-and-Breakfast   36
Saddle Rock Ranch   38

CENTRAL ARIZONA

Jerome

Ghost City Inn Bed-and-Breakfast   45

Inn at Jerome   47

Jerome Grand Hotel   49

The Surgeon's House Bed-and-Breakfast   51

Prescott

Hassayampa Inn   54

Hotel St. Michael   56

Hotel Vendome   59

The Marks House   61

Mount Vernon Inn   63

Pleasant Street Inn Bed-and-Breakfast   66

Prescott Pines Inn   68

Victorian Inn of Prescott   71

White Mountains
Lakeside / Pinetop

The Coldstream Bed-and-Breakfast   73

Lakeview Lodge   76

Greer

Molly Butler Lodge   78

White Mountain Lodge   80

Eagar / Springerville

Paisley Corner Bed-and-Breakfast   83

Alpine

Hannagan Meadow Lodge   85

Wickenburg
Kay El Bar Guest Ranch   88
Sombrero Ranch Bed-and-Breakfast   91

Litchfield Park
The Wigwam Resort   93

Scottsdale
Marriott's Camelback Inn   96

Paradise Valley
Hermosa Inn   98

Phoenix
Arizona Biltmore   101
Maricopa Manor Bed-and-Breakfast Inn   103
Royal Palms   106
San Carlos Hotel   109

Mesa
Saguaro Lake Ranch Resort   111

Chandler
San Marcos Resort   114

Globe
Noftsger Hill Inn   116

SOUTHERN ARIZONA

Florence
Inn at Rancho Sonora   123

Taylor's Bed-and-Breakfast   125

Safford
Olney House Bed-and-Breakfast   127

Oracle
Triangle L Ranch   129

Yuma
Best Western Coronado Motor Hotel   132

Ajo
The Guest House Inn   134
The Mine Manager's House Inn   137

Tucson
Adobe Rose Inn Bed-and-Breakfast   139
Arizona Inn   141
Casa Alegre Bed-and-Breakfast Inn   144
Catalina Park Inn   146
Copper Bell Bed-and-Breakfast   148
El Presidio Bed-and-Breakfast Inn   150
Elysian Grove Market Bed-and-Breakfast Inn   153
Hacienda del Sol Guest Ranch Resort   155
Hotel Congress   157
La Posada del Valle   160
Lazy K Bar Guest Ranch   162
The Lodge on the Desert   165
Peppertrees Bed-and-Breakfast Inn   167
Tanque Verde Ranch   170
Westward Look Resort   172
White Stallion Guest Ranch   175
Wild Horse Ranch Resort   177

Willcox
Muleshoe Ranch   179

Dragoon
Triangle T Guest Ranch   182

Tombstone
Buford House   184
Priscilla's Bed-and-Breakfast   186
Tombstone Boarding House Bed-and-Breakfast Inn   188
Victoria's Bed-and-Breakfast   190

Amado
Rex Ranch   192

Tubac / Tumacacori
Valle Verde Ranch Bed-and-Breakfast   195

Sonoita
The Vineyard Bed-and-Breakfast   197

Patagonia
Circle Z Ranch   199
The Duquesne House Bed-and-Breakfast   202

Sasabe
Rancho de la Osa   204

Hereford
San Pedro River Inn   207

Bisbee

Bisbee Grand Hotel   209

Bisbee Inn   211

Calumet & Arizona Guest House   213

Clawson House   216

Copper Queen Hotel   218

High Desert Inn   220

Inn at Castle Rock   222

Judge Ross House   224

Main Street Inn   226

OK Street Jailhouse   228

Oliver House   230

School House Inn   232

Douglas

Gadsden Hotel   234

Index   237

Acknowledgments

SPECIAL THANKS GO TO

Ruth Long at Mi Casa-Su Casa for her helpful support

The Arizona Office of Tourism, the State Historic Preservation Office,
and the Arizona Dude Ranch Association,
for providing necessary information and assistance

The various chambers of commerce, historical societies, and visitor
bureaus, for providing important material on their particular cities

The owners, innkeepers, and managers of these historic structures, for
their interest and enthusiasm for this project and for generously sharing
their establishments' history

My supportive family and cherished friends near and far,
who graciously tolerate my travel addiction

My editor, Steve Kirk, for his faith and patience

Introduction

IN TODAY'S HURRIED, HIGH-TECH WORLD, more and more travelers are seeking an escape from the frenzy and stress of modern life.
They are weary of look-alike buildings that seem a little too sleek and
people who rush by, too busy to smile. Many yearn for an escape to a
place with character and an interesting history. They want to return for a
while to a time when the pace was slower and people friendlier.

Across Arizona's breathtaking landscape lies a fascinating collection of
preserved historic structures ranging from turreted Victorians and bawdy
bordellos to rustic dude ranches and quaint mountain lodges, from haunted
boardinghouses and authentic trading posts to classic Southwestern adobes and glamorous resorts. The 94 accommodations featured in this book
are as broad and colorful as the state itself and as diverse as the people
who shaped its history.

Arizona is an ancient land where prehistoric Hohokam and Anasazi Indians carved their dwellings into the sides of sandstone cliffs more than
8,000 years ago. Spanish explorers arrived in the mid-1500s, searching
for fabled cities of gold. Next came missionaries from Mexico, followed

by miners, cowboys, cattlemen, and cotton farmers. As new settlers arrived, towns and cities emerged across the landscape. Some faded into obscurity and became ghost towns, others survived and prospered.

Many of the state's earliest buildings were lost in devastating fires that swept through booming mining and railroad towns. Others fell to the wrecking ball in the name of progress. But some managed to escape destruction and demolition and were saved for posterity through restoration by preservation-minded owners. Many of these historic structures provide accommodations to the public and offer today's traveler a unique glimpse into Arizona's past.

The inviting inns, lodges, hotels, and resorts in this book are located all across the state, from the magnificent Grand Canyon and haunting Canyon de Chelly in the north to arid saguaro-studded deserts in the south. There are glamorous old hotels like the San Carlos Hotel in Phoenix, the Hotel Congress in Tucson, and the Copper Queen in Bisbee, which were built to serve as centers of activity during their towns' heyday and remain valuable treasures of history today.

In Prescott, streets in the historic district are lined with stately Victorians topped with turrets and trimmed in gingerbread, reminders of the town's Midwestern heritage. Some, converted into bed-and-breakfasts, offer stressed-out travelers a return to the early 20th century in beautifully restored rooms filled with elegant antiques. A block or so away, at Courthouse Plaza, passersby can rest on a park bench and enjoy the small-town flavor of Arizona's first territorial capital.

Arizona's wild Old West image is kept alive in Tombstone, where the famous 1881 gunfight in which the Earp brothers and Doc Holliday shot it out with the Clanton Gang is reenacted regularly at the OK Corral, located a few blocks from the quaint bed-and-breakfasts featured in this book.

In Bisbee, travelers can actually "do time" in an authentic jail at the High Desert Inn and the OK Street Jailhouse. These restored structures feature original cells, jail doors, and bars over the windows.

Many establishments have appeared in movies and were occupied by stars and film crews, beginning with the first silent productions. Tom Mix, one of the first silent-screen cowboys, was known to hold court in the lobby of the Hassayampa Inn in Prescott. John Wayne preferred the room nearest the bar at the Copper Queen Hotel in Bisbee. The Saddle Rock Ranch, which sits on a slope overlooking the red rocks of Sedona, provided the setting for several Western films and hosted the likes of Jimmy Stewart, Randolph Scott, and Hopalong Cassidy. In downtown Flagstaff, the Monte Vista Hotel once served as a home away from home for novelist Zane Grey and also opened its doors to big-name stars like Humphrey Bogart, Jane Russell, and Clark Gable. The ornate Gadsden Hotel in Douglas, a longtime attraction for filmmakers, was featured in *The Life and Times of Judge Roy Bean* and has appeared in numerous documentaries and television productions. Tucson, with its Old Tucson Film Studios tucked among saguaros and mountain foothills west of town, stands out as the leader in film production. More than 200 movies, commercials, documentaries, and television shows have been filmed at this "Hollywood in the Desert," built in 1939 as a set for the movie *Arizona*.

Glamorous resorts began emerging around the state during the 1920s and 1930s. The first public resort was the San Marcos, built in 1912, the year Arizona was granted statehood. Erected in Chandler, then a remote farming community south of Phoenix, the elegant hotel became a desert playground for celebrities, dignitaries, and socialites. Another famous resort that grew into a world-class escape for the famous and well heeled is the Arizona Biltmore in Phoenix. Inspired by architect Frank Lloyd Wright, this unique concrete structure was owned by Chicago chewing-gum magnate William Wrigley, Jr., and has the distinction of having hosted every United States president since its opening in 1930. The historic Camelback Inn in Scottsdale—where the saying "Where Time Stands Still" continues to hang above the entrance—so impressed the family of hotel baron J. W. Marriott, Sr., that Marriott later purchased the inn and continues its operation today. The Westward Look Resort in Tucson, the town's oldest resort, was built in 1912 as a remote adobe family residence far from town. The city eventually crawled up the foothills of the Santa

Catalina Mountains and enclosed the resort, but the Westward Look continues to reign as a luxurious desert escape.

The celebration of the Old West flourished in the 1930s and 1940s, when dude ranches began appearing on the landscape. Travelers from around the world began coming to Arizona to live out their cowboy and cowgirl dreams at rustic guest ranches in Tucson and Wickenburg. At the Tanque Verde Ranch in Tucson, it's a common occurrence to hear a variety of languages spoken, especially during the summer, when guests from Europe and Japan don 10-gallon hats and cowboy boots and ride off into the sunset.

Some accommodations in this book are located in modest structures. Others are former residences of ordinary citizens who contributed to their towns' development. The Molly Butler Lodge, a wooden, shingle-roofed structure in the picturesque White Mountains village of Greer, is Arizona's oldest guest lodge. It began as the homestead of a pioneering family who arrived in the area in the 1890s. The Birch Tree Inn, a two-story clapboard home built in 1916 of simple box design, features Victorian enhancements like leaded-glass windows, French doors, and large bay windows, a look befitting its former owner, the town's mayor.

While working on this book, I was often asked how I determined a structure's merit. Basically, there were three main requirements for inclusion. First, to be considered historic, the building had to be at least a half-century old—the older, the better. The featured establishments all contain structures dating to 1940 or earlier, although many have been enlarged and updated through the years. The second requirement was that the establishment offer accommodations to the general public. The third was that I must personally visit each structure. Architectural character and distinctive features were other considerations. Many of the structures are listed on the National Register of Historic Places and have been recognized as historically significant by various national, state, and local historic-preservation organizations. A building's role in its town's development was also considered.

Each accommodation in this book offers a particular reward to the interested guest. The small inns, bed-and-breakfasts, and mountain lodges are usually the friendliest and warmest. Most feature an inviting parlor or gathering room, usually set in front of a fireplace, where guests can converse, share experiences, and become friends, even for only a day. Because I'm convinced that the best way to get to know a particular area is through the people who live there, I find innkeepers a wealth of information. They are knowledgeable about the history of their homes as well as their town and are prepared to answer your questions and provide suggestions on dining, shopping, and sightseeing. They also try very hard not to intrude, if it's privacy you seek. Many innkeepers are excellent cooks and quite accommodating when it comes to special dietary breakfast needs. All they need is a little advance notice.

The large establishments—the guest ranches, hotels, and resorts—have well-trained staff members who take pride in the historic value of their structure and are eager to answer your questions about its history and the surrounding area. These self-contained operations normally house restaurants or dining rooms and gift shops. Because historic hotels are usually located downtown in the town's historic district, a wonderful opportunity exists to explore the surrounding streets and steep oneself in the town's history.

Because this book is subjective, not every historic establishment is included. Some worthy candidates were in transition and unable to participate, and others were not interested.

In order to guarantee a memorable escape, it is best to plan ahead. Most inns, ranches, and resorts do not allow pets, although there are a few that accept them if they are well behaved and not too large. Smoking is rarely allowed indoors, but many establishments permit smoking in designated areas outdoors. Quoting specific room rates would in many cases make this book obsolete before it was printed, so I have listed rate ranges instead. Many Arizona accommodations feature seasonal rates, which can vary dramatically, especially at resorts and guest ranches. Room rates at bed-and-breakfasts and small inns usually include breakfast. Guest ranches operate on the American plan, which normally includes three substantial meals per day, plus the use of the facilities. Large resorts and hotels usually have full-service in-house restaurants and bars. Unless otherwise stated, rooms rates are for two persons, but it is always best to contact the establishment for the most current information.

Reservations are recommended for all of the accommodations in this book, especially during peak travel periods, weekends, and holidays. A deposit of one night's lodging is required at most inns, and many require a minimum stay of two nights on weekends. Do not expect a deposit refund if you cancel at the last minute. However, with notice of a week or more, efforts will be made to rerent your room and refund your deposit. Check-in time is usually mid- to late afternoon, with departure expected before noon. Some of the smaller inns do not accept credit cards, so be sure to check with the innkeeper.

It is my hope that this book will serve as an entertaining travel guide to Arizona's fascinating historic accommodations, where you can escape today's hectic pace and relax, turn back the clock, and discover the past. Whether your ideal getaway is a cozy rock cottage in Sedona, a five-star resort in Phoenix, or a rustic guest ranch in Tucson, wonderful escapes await you.

Saddle Rock Ranch,
Sedona

Arizona's

Historic

Escapes

NORTHERN ARIZONA

Grand Canyon
Canyon de Chelly
Flagstaff
Sedona

FEW STATES CAN CLAIM such a spectacular and varied landscape as Arizona.

Millions of travelers from all over the globe visit northern Arizona each year to stare into the multihued layers of the **Grand Canyon**, one of the Seven Natural Wonders of the World. Many writers, artists, and photographers have tried to describe its awesome beauty, but this incredible gorge must be seen. Carved through the ages by the Colorado River, the canyon is over 2 billion years old and measures a mile deep and 277 miles long.

Tourists began arriving at the canyon's South Rim in the late 1800s, when transportation consisted of a bumpy stagecoach ride from Flagstaff. Accommodations were provided in tents. By 1901, passengers were rolling into the log depot in Grand Canyon Village on steam trains from downtown **Williams**, which calls itself the "Gateway to the Canyon." The historic trains, restored and returned to service as the Grand Canyon Railway in 1989, provide a scenic ride through pine forests and meadows to the canyon's South Rim.

The northeastern portion of the state belongs to the Navajo Nation and the Hopi Indian Reservation, the largest Native American reservation in the country. Home of the unforgettable **Canyon de Chelly**, it is a hauntingly beautiful land of towering red buttes, barren plains, broad mesas, and sandstone cliffs where ancient Anasazis once lived. It is an area rich in cultural traditions, where Native Americans continue the lessons of their ancestors today. Their distinctive pottery, weavings, and jewelry can be purchased at various locations, including historic trading posts.

Pine-studded **Flagstaff** has long been a stopover for travelers. Because of the profusion of fast-food restaurants and flashing neon signs, many visitors miss the frontier flavor of the downtown historic area, with its many turn-of-the-century buildings. The town's location at the base of the snow-capped San Francisco Peaks, Arizona's highest mountains, makes it a skiers' paradise in winter and a cool summertime escape for sunscorched Phoenicians.

The giant red-rock formations of **Sedona** are located 20 miles south of Flagstaff. The drive along US 89A through Oak Creek Canyon is one of state's most scenic. Once a remote artists' colony and a popular setting for Western movies in the 1940s and 1950s, Sedona has grown at a tremendous rate during the past decade. It is sometimes compared to Santa Fe because of its many galleries, shops, and restaurants.

Things to do and see

GRAND CANYON VILLAGE, South Rim

National Park Service Visitor Center. Located on the rim walk, the visitor center offers a wide range of information, including movies, maps, books, tours, hikes, and lectures.

Hopi House. This well-stocked gift shop sells Native American crafts. It is housed in a striking multilevel rock-and-mortar structure modeled after Hopi Indian ruins at Oraibi.

Lookout Studio. This museum, gift shop, and lookout point is in a 1914 structure resembling a Hopi pueblo. It was designed by Mary Jane Colter, an architect for the Fred Harvey Company.

The Watchtower. Built in 1932, this 70-foot stone-and-mortar watchtower is located at the end of a 25-mile drive along the South Rim to Desert View. It offers breathtaking views of the Painted Desert and the Colorado River, as well as galleries and a gift shop selling Native American crafts.

NAVAJO-HOPI COUNTRY

Chinle. This is the closest town to Canyon de Chelly, one of the Southwest's most spectacular national monuments. The 26-mile-long Canyon de Chelly (pronounced Canyon d' Shay) and the 35-mile-long Canyon del Muerto are breathtaking, with prehistoric ruins and sandstone walls that soar upward 1,000 feet, revealing ancient pictographs. Visitors can explore the area by car or with guides on foot, or they can sign up for a truck or jeep tour at the visitor center in Chinle. For information, call 520-674-5500.

FLAGSTAFF

Riordan State Historic Park. Visitors can see the 40-room log-and-stone mansion built in 1904 for the lumber baron Riordan brothers during Flagstaff's logging heyday. The architect was Charles Whittlesley, who also designed El Tovar at the Grand Canyon. Call 520-779-4395 for tour times and fees.

SEDONA

Chapel of the Holy Cross. This contemporary structure soars upward between two red-rock peaks. Built by Marguerite Staude, a Frank Lloyd Wright disciple, it features a huge cross and provides vistas of the town. It is located off Chapel Road on AZ 179 a few miles south of town.

Tlaquepaque (pronounced Tuh-la-kay-pah-kay). This is a re-created Old World Mexican village, with tiled courtyards, fountains, cafes, quality art galleries, and gift shops.

Oak Creek Canyon. Visitors should take the winding drive along US 89A north toward Flagstaff, through deep canyons with dramatic rock formations and views of Oak Creek, which runs along the bottom of the canyon.

Bright Angel Lodge

Bright Angel Lodge

Grand Canyon National Park Lodges
Box 699
Grand Canyon, Arizona 86023
phone: 303-29PARKS or 520-638-2631
fax: 303-297-3175

BACK IN THE 1890s, visitors arrived at the Grand Canyon by stage-coach after a long and bumpy ride from Flagstaff that included three stops for changing horses. The travelers were weary and in need of overnight lodging, a situation which prompted the stage-line owner, J. Wilbur Thurber, to open his Bright Angel Hotel in 1896.

Hotel was hardly the proper name for the primitive accommodations, which included an assortment of tents and a single cabin that served as an office. The misnomer was corrected in 1905, when the Fred Harvey Company assumed management of the Grand Canyon Village facilities and promptly renamed the primitive quarters Bright Angel Camp.

Considered unsightly by 1935, the original camp was replaced by the present structure and given the name Bright Angel Lodge. It was designed by architect Mary Jane Colter, whose work emphasizes nature's beauty over human works. Although she is responsible for a number of the area's historic landmarks, the Bright Angel Lodge is considered Colter's ultimate Grand Canyon achievement.

The Pioneer-style main lodge, constructed of native boulders and logs, is a short walk for passengers arriving at the 1901 depot on the authentic steam-powered Grand Canyon Railway. The handsome lobby features sturdy log furniture and walls, a soaring ceiling, flagstone floors, and an enormous stone fireplace. Above the mantel hangs a striking wooden thunderbird, a mythical figure in American Indian lore said to cause thunder and lightning.

The History Room, to the left of the main lobby, has large windows overlooking the canyon's rim. It features a "geological" fireplace of canyon rocks arranged in their proper stratigraphic sequence. The room also houses an interesting exhibit about Fred Harvey, whose company has been the primary concessionaire on the South Rim since the 1920s. Harvey, an immigrant from England, is credited by some with civilizing the West with his good food and refined service, presented by the pretty, prim, and proper "Harvey Girls." The historic main lodge also includes two restaurants, a cocktail lounge offering live entertainment, and a gift shop. It can resemble a mob scene, especially during the busy summer months.

The Bright Angel Lodge is open all year. It offers a choice of rustic accommodations. Guests may stay in comfortable rooms in the main lodge or select one of the more camplike log-and-stone cabins scattered among the tall pines or overlooking the rim. Some rooms include fireplaces, wall-to-wall carpeting, wood paneling, and private baths, while others offer efficient dormitory-style accommodations and shared baths. All rooms are clean, comfortable, and modestly furnished. They blend beautifully into the splendid Grand Canyon landscape, just as Mary Jane Colter envisioned.

Rates

Standard rooms (single or double) are available for $53, historic cabins for $61, and rim cabins for $89 to $111. Some have private baths; others are dormitory-style with a shared bath. Advance reservations are recommended, especially for the summer season. No pets are allowed. American Express, Diners Club, MasterCard, and Visa are accepted.

Amenities

Some cabins have fireplaces. A coffee shop, a snack shop, a restaurant, a lounge, a gift shop, and a museum are in the main lodge. The lodge is within walking distance of the train depot.

Location

The lodge is at the South Rim of the Grand Canyon.

El Tovar Hotel

Grand Canyon National Park Lodges
Box 699
Grand Canyon, Arizona 86023
phone: 303-29PARKS or 520-638-2631
fax: 303-297-3175

LUXURY FINALLY ARRIVED at the Grand Canyon in 1905, when construction on El Tovar Hotel was completed. Passenger trains had been journeying to the canyon's South Rim for four years, and the time seemed right to provide travelers with a first-class lodging and dining establishment.

El Tovar Hotel was financed by the Fred Harvey Company and constructed by the Santa Fe Railroad. Architect Charles Whittlesley was instructed to design a hotel that would blend into its surroundings and not detract from the canyon's grandeur. He met the challenge by combining the characteristics of a Swiss chalet and a Norwegian villa, utilizing native stone, hand-peeled Oregon pine, and Douglas fir. The result was a sprawling multilevel hotel which resembles a European hunting lodge, with wooden columns, curved railings, balconies, and spacious verandas.

The hotel was named after Spanish explorer Don Pedro de Tovar, who discovered the area in 1540 while searching for the legendary Seven Cities of Cibola. Called "the architectural crown jewel of the Grand Canyon," El Tovar Hotel was a showplace from the start, offering a variety of luxurious amenities. Along with canyon views, guests could enjoy electric lights powered by a steam generator, solariums, music rooms, and fresh water hauled by railroad from a point 120 miles away. A dairy and greenhouses on the premises provided milk products and fresh fruit and vegetables. Under the expert management of the Fred Harvey Company since its beginning, El Tovar has been designated a National Historic Site and reigns as one of the grand old hotels of the West.

El Tovar Hotel

Perched majestically near the canyon's South Rim, the hotel looks much as it did early in the 20th century. It continues to offer guests from all over the globe deluxe accommodations and a spectacular view of one of the wonders of the world, that multicolored gorge 10 miles wide and a mile deep, formed millions of years ago by the Colorado River.

The handsome main lobby features dark pine-log walls and columns, copper chandeliers, rustic furnishings, a massive stone fireplace, and mounted animal heads. Upstairs overlooking the lobby is a comfortable octagonal lounge—the former women's lobby—where afternoon tea is still served. The hotel offers 65 guest rooms, including 10 suites which have been refurbished through the years to maintain their original charm. Each room has been updated to include modern conveniences such as private baths and is decorated with period furnishings.

The hotel's dining room, located at the rear of the lobby, reflects the refined rusticity and genteel hospitality launched long ago by the famous "Harvey Girls." These proper young ladies, imported from the East and outfitted in prim black dresses with white aprons and collars, set the standard for the elegant service which continues today. The tables are formally dressed with fine linens, sparkling crystal, and elegant china. The exquisite continental cuisine is sure to please the international palates of the canyon's many visitors.

Because El Tovar Hotel would not exist if not for the scenic wonder of the Grand Canyon, the hotel does its very best to make the canyon view available by serving meals from early morning to late evening.

Rates

The rooms are available for $115 to $175 and the suites for $200 to $300. Reservations are recommended, especially in summer. Meals are not included. No pets are allowed in the rooms, but kennels are available. Credit cards are accepted.

Amenities
Phones and televisions are in all rooms. A lounge, a restaurant, a gift shop, and a concierge are provided.

Location
The hotel is at the South Rim of the Grand Canyon in Grand Canyon Village.

Chinle

Thunderbird Lodge
P.O. Box 548
Chinle, Arizona 86503
phone: 520-674-5841
fax: 520-674-5844
Mary Jones, owner

TOURISTS COME FROM ALL OVER the world to stare in wonder at Arizona's great canyons, where prehistoric nomads once roamed. One of the Southwest's most spectacular national monuments is the haunting Canyon de Chelly, located on the Navajo Indian Reservation in northeastern Arizona. It is the land where Anasazi Indians lived before vanishing around the year 1300, leaving behind stone cliff dwellings and ancient pictographs on 1,000-foot-high sandstone walls and giant stone formations. Today, the land belongs to the Navajo, some of whom raise sheep and farm the fertile area between the rugged cliffs, much like their ancestors who settled in the area around 1700. Other Navajo staff and operate the motels and lodges

Thunderbird Lodge

that have sprung up during the past few decades to accommodate the area's growing number of visitors. Many guests book a room at the site where the area's first tourists stayed, the historic Thunderbird Lodge, located at the mouth of the ancient Canyon de Chelly.

The story of the Thunderbird Lodge began in 1902, when a civil engineer named Sam Day erected a rectangular adobe structure 60 feet wide by 20 feet deep to serve as a trading post for the widely scattered Navajo. A few years later, Day sold the trading post to new owners, who enlarged it and built a stone-and-adobe ranch house nearby.

But it wasn't until 1919, when Leon "Cozy" McSparron purchased the property and named it the Thunderbird Ranch, that tourists began to notice. Cozy's tireless promotion of the area's wonders began to reach travelers eager to experience the Canyon de Chelly's grandeur. After traveling unpaved roads, they arrived at the trading post needing accommodations. Cozy set out a few cots around the post. Then, as business grew, he added cabins and a residence for himself. The enterprising Cozy also organized the first tours into the canyon, using horses and wagons initially and Model-T Fords later. His efforts to promote Navajo woven goods and silversmithing eventually helped to earn the Canyon de Chelly's designation as a National Monument in 1931.

Failing health forced Cozy to sell the ranch in 1954, and the trading post and lodge changed hands again. The lodge was given a new name, old rooms were remodeled, and new guest facilities were added to serve the growing horde of visitors. In 1969, the old trading post was converted into a cafeteria. More guest rooms were added when present owner Mary Jones purchased the ranch in 1984 and renamed it the Thunderbird Lodge.

Giant cottonwood trees planted in the 1940s tower over the sprawling lodge and its landscaped grounds. The original ranch house now has a layer of flagstone on its exterior walls. It serves as the canyon-tour office and gift shop. The stone guest cottages sit behind the gift shop a short walk from the old tin-roofed trading post.

The new guest rooms added at the rear of the property in the 1980s reflect the Pueblo-style architecture of the area. The decor throughout the lodge is rustic Southwestern, with comfortable furnishings and attractive Navajo print bedspreads and wall hangings. Staffed by knowledgeable Navajo willing to share information on canyon tours and hikes, Native American performances, and various nature programs, the lodge is a center for area activities.

Rates

The 72 rooms with private baths are available for $79 to $88. The lodge is open all year. No pets are allowed. Smoking is not permitted indoors.
Meals are not included. Major credit cards are accepted.

Amenities

The rooms have cable television and phones.
A cafeteria, a gift shop, and canyon tours are available.

Location

The lodge is 3.5 miles east of US 191 in Canyon de Chelly National Monument, just south of the visitor center.

The Johnstonian Bed-and-Breakfast

The Johnstonian Bed-and-Breakfast

321 West Sheridan Avenue
Williams, Arizona 86046
phone: 520-635-2178
Bill and Pidge Johnston, owners/innkeepers

THE JOHNSTONIAN BED-AND-BREAKFAST was built in 1900, a year before the completion of a 60-mile railroad spur line earned Williams the nickname "Gateway to the Grand Canyon." In 1901, passenger trains began steaming out of Williams, chugging through grassy plains and ponderosa pine forests to the South Rim of the Grand Canyon. The steam trains operated until 1968, when they came to a halt that lasted for 21 years. Service was restored in 1989. Passengers can once again climb aboard authentically restored 1923 Harriman coaches pulled by turn-of-the-century steam engines or vintage diesel locomotives and arrive at the Grand Canyon's 1910 log depot in historic style.

Travelers wanting to keep that turn-of-the-century feeling alive will enjoy a stay at the Johnstonian Bed-and-Breakfast, a bright blue Victorian with white shutters, gingerbread trim, and a red roof. The romantic two-story cottage is tucked primly behind a white picket fence on a quiet neighborhood street.

Bill and Pidge Johnston, the friendly innkeepers and owners, have carefully restored and furnished their historic home in the style of the period with antique oak furnishings, floral wall coverings, and dainty lace curtains. Through the years, modern comforts have been added, but the focus at the Johnstonian is on the past. Original floors of native pine and fir, old-time light fixtures, and a 1929 piano from the Bright Angel Lodge are a few of the items that have pleased guests from over 46 countries.

The wood stove in the dining room is a favorite gathering spot in the winter, when the aroma of Pidge's homemade bread drifting in from the nearby kitchen is sure to bring back memories of a cozy day at Grandma's house. Breakfast—another nostalgia-producing event—features Ukrainian potato cakes, pecan waffles, apple-blueberry pancakes, and steaming cups of coffee and is served at the round oak dining table.

The guests rooms, located on both levels, have the same old-fashioned furnishings found throughout the rest of the house. The downstairs guest room comes with a private bath. Upstairs, three rooms share a bath. The Johnstonian's location—only an hour's drive from the Grand Canyon—makes this a convenient off-the-beaten-path escape from the motel-lined main thoroughfare in Williams, which is often crowded with visitors traveling to and from the canyon.

Rates

Rooms are available for $45 to $110 (for the suite). A full sit-down breakfast is included. Children are welcome. No pets are allowed. Cash, personal checks, and traveler's checks are accepted, but credit cards are not. Check-in is at 3 P.M. and check-out at 10 A.M.

Amenities

One of the four rooms has a private bath; the other three share a bath. Guests enjoy the quiet neighborhood. Television and a house phone are available.

Red Garter Bed-and-Bakery

137 West Railroad Avenue
Williams, Arizona 86046
phone: 800-328-1484 or 520-635-1484
John W. Holst, innkeeper

BACK IN 1897, an ambitious tailor named August Tetzlaff built a two-story saloon and bordello on "Saloon Row" in downtown Williams. His aim was to satisfy the needs of the loggers, cowboys, and railroad workers who had settled in the frontier town. The building was constructed in the Victorian Romanesque style and included a cast-iron cornice shipped by rail from the East. The sturdy cornice is credited with stopping the great fires of 1901 and 1903, which destroyed most of the other buildings on the block. The original keystone with Tetzlaff's name and the building's construction date is still in position above the arched entrance and the red-and-white sign announcing the building's newest role, that of a bed-and-breakfast inn and small bakery.

The town's fallen angels no longer wave from the second-story bordello's windows, which overlook the train tracks across the street. Gone also are the back-room poker games, the Chinese restaurant and opium den, and the two-story outhouse.

The century-old building, listed on the National Register of Historic Places, has been creatively restored by John Holst, who reopened it as the Red Garter Bed-and-Bakery in 1994. The entrance to the former bordello is located downstairs beside the front door to the bakery. A floral-carpeted stairway leads to the eight former "cribs" and the madam's room upstairs, which have been cleverly transformed into a quaint, inviting inn with a cozy central parlor and four guest rooms. All the rooms have private baths, 12-foot ceilings, over-the-door transoms, and romantic 1890s Victorian decor with original skylights, period furnishings, and lace curtains. The largest and most popular room in the house is the Honeymoon Suite, which has a sitting room and windows overlooking a pine forest and the railroad tracks, used regularly by restored steam trains chugging to and from the Grand Canyon.

Restoration of the ground-floor bakery, which doubles as the inn's lobby and breakfast area, was completed in the spring of 1995. Where liquor was once dispensed in the former saloon, delicious home-baked goodies are now served in a cozy cafe. Amid gleaming wood floors, oak-beam ceilings, and a colorful wall mural of a cowboy cattle drive, guests and locals mingle and munch on the bakery's delicious cinnamon rolls, croissants, and fruit-and-nut-filled muffins, fresh from the oven.

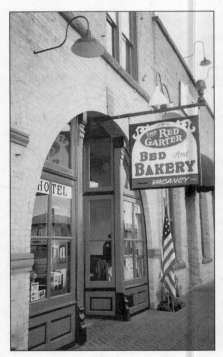

Red Garter Bed-and-Bakery

Rates

The four rooms (including one two-room suite) are available for $45 to $85. Seasonal rates apply; high season is May through September. Continental breakfast is included.

Amenities

The rooms have private baths. Guests may enjoy color cable television in the parlor. A guest telephone is provided. Ice is adjacent to the rooms. A small gift shop is in the bakery.

Location

The building is on West Railroad Avenue (Old Route 66) across the street from the Grand Canyon Railway tracks.

Birch Tree Inn

824 West Birch Avenue
Flagstaff, Arizona 86001
phone: 800-645-5805 or 520-774-1042
Donna and Rodger Pettinger and Sandy and Ed Znetko, innkeepers

THE STORY OF THE BIRCH TREE INN began in 1916, when the Rosen family from Chicago started construction on a home at the end of Birch Street a few blocks from downtown Flagstaff. Using native volcanic rock for the foundation, the Rosens erected a two-story clapboard home of simple box design with a wraparound porch, classical columns, and a low-pitched roof. Although not a mansion, the home included many elegant Victorian enhancements and occupied a site spanning three city lots. When completed in 1917, the spacious structure with leaded-glass windows, French doors, a large bay window, and a library resembled a stately country manor befitting a lord—or perhaps a local politician.

Birch Tree Inn

In 1929, Joseph Waldhous, Flagstaff's mayor, purchased the home, where he continued to live until 1967. Afterwards, it was used for five years as a fraternity house for students at nearby Northern Arizona University. In 1988, two couples from California, Donna and Rodger Pettinger and Sandy and Ed Znetko, purchased the historic home, the only remaining building on the block dating to the 1920s. They converted it into a bright and cheerful bed-and-breakfast.

Look for the inviting white clapboard house with blue trim across from a city park and Coconino National Forest at the end of Birch Street. The wide wraparound porch is a welcome sight indeed for guests looking to unwind in Flagstaff's pine-scented country. Inside, refreshments wait in front of the brick fireplace within view of the billiard table in the adjoining bay-windowed game room.

The inn's five guest rooms are located at the top of a gleaming oak staircase. Each is decorated according to a different theme. Three rooms have private baths and two share a bath. From the two windows in the corner Wicker Room, guests have a view of the San Francisco Peaks, Arizona's highest mountain range. The white-and-blue Pella Room is a Dutch delight with handmade quilt, wooden shoes, and lace curtains. The corner Southwest Suite, the original master bedroom, is the largest room; its highlights are a king-size bed with a stucco headboard and a spacious bath that formerly served as the family bathroom. Carol's Room features Shaker pine furnishings and a view of the park and the forest. The Wagner-Znetko Room has cheerful yellow decor and an antique sewing machine and rocking chair.

Late-afternoon tea and snacks are served in the high-ceilinged parlor. In the morning, guests enjoy a full breakfast served with china and silver in the dining room downstairs or on the veranda. Frequent requests for the hosts' delicious breakfast recipes have led to the publication of a cookbook featuring items served at the inn. The friendly innkeepers are happy to assist with dinner and sightseeing reservations.

Rates

The five rooms are available for $60 to $89. One suite is offered; two rooms have private baths, and two share a bath. Full breakfast is included. Reservations may be guaranteed with Visa, MasterCard, or American Express. No children under 10 or pets are allowed. Smoking is not permitted indoors.

Amenities

A guest phone is downstairs, and a television is in the parlor. Guests may also enjoy billiards and a piano.

Location

The inn is near historic downtown Flagstaff. From US 180, turn west on Birch Avenue and drive six blocks. The inn is on the right at the end of the street.

Dierker House Bed-and-Breakfast

423 West Cherry Street
Flagstaff, Arizona 86001
phone: 520-774-3249
Dorothea Dierker, owner/innkeeper

FLAGSTAFF'S FIRST PERMANENT SETTLER, a Tennessean who arrived in 1876 with a herd of sheep, set the stage for other sheepherding families who eventually followed his lead. A dozen years later, more than 200,000 sheep grazed the lands of northern Arizona and were producing 2 million pounds of fleece a season. Many sheepherding families built summer homes in the pine-studded forests near town. Among them were the LaBarons, who chose to erect their summer residence on a heavily wooded site on the corner of Park and Cherry Streets in 1914.

With a solid rock foundation and a rugged rock fireplace, the frame

Dierker House Bed-and-Breakfast

structure was built to last. Dottie Dierker, who has owned the house for the past 45 years, can attest to its soundness. After all, she raised six strapping sons—all former boatmen on the Colorado River—and opened the upstairs as a bed-and-breakfast in 1983. She claims it's the oldest continuously operating bed-and-breakfast in Flagstaff.

It's no surprise to hear that the pale green cottage nestled under a canopy of towering trees is a favorite of Europeans. With its home-in-the-forest appeal and convenient location in a residential neighborhood a few blocks from historic downtown Flagstaff, it's sure to please travelers far from their homeland. There's also the wide porch that stretches across the entire front of the house like the smile on the face of owner/innkeeper Dottie, a retired nurse who can't seem to stop tending to the needs of others.

A private staircase leads to the second-floor accommodations, which include a small gathering area, a kitchenette, a bath, and three guest rooms. The rooms are named France, Germany, and Greece and are decorated accordingly. A comfortable, homey feeling exists throughout the entire upstairs, where guests have the run of the floor. And they are also welcome downstairs, where Dottie lives, raises orchids, cares for her dogs and rooms full of antiques, and prepares those delicious country breakfasts. No doubt, the most popular room is the spacious, plant-filled garden room at the back of the house. This is where canaries chirp in cages, where ferns drip from hanging pots, where the pool table stands ready, and where a familiar old tune plays away on the authentic Wurlitzer jukebox. Whatever the reason, visitors seem to find their way back to the Dierker House Bed-and-Breakfast.

Rates

The three rooms, which share a bath, are available for $50 and up. Breakfast is included. No children under 12 or pets are allowed. Smoking is not permitted indoors. Cash and checks are accepted, but credit cards are not.

Amenities

Television, a refrigerator in the common area, and a large front porch are available to guests.

Location

The house is in downtown Flagstaff at the corner of Cherry and Park Streets, three blocks north of Route 66.

Hotel Monte Vista

100 North San Francisco Street
Flagstaff, Arizona 86001
phone: 800-545-3068 or 520-779-6971
fax: 520-779-2904

NO, GEORGE WASHINGTON didn't sleep at this landmark hotel, but Teddy Roosevelt, Jane Russell, Gary Cooper, Carole Lombard, Humphrey

Hotel Monte Vista

Bogart, Alan Ladd, and Barbara Stanwyck did. Such glamorous Holly-wood stars and other notables stayed at the Monte Vista during the 1930s and 1940s, when over a hundred Western movies were filmed in and around the area. Top-notch accommodations were few and far between then, and the Monte Vista soon became a home away from home for cele-brities and for travelers motoring along Route 66. This historic route, which opened in Flagstaff in 1926, stretched from the Midwest to the West Coast, bringing scores of travelers into Flagstaff until the mid-1980s, when the city was bypassed by Interstate 40.

When tourism was on the rise in the mid-1920s, local citizens agreed the time was right for Flagstaff to have a first-class hotel. In 1926, an impressive four-story structure of brick, steel, and concrete was erected on a corner in the heart of town. Novelist Zane Grey put up half the money, and most of the town's prominent citizens also invested in the venture. The hotel's original name, the Flagstaff Community Hotel, appears in several novels penned by Grey during his frequent stays. It was renamed when Monte Vista (Spanish for "mountain view") was selected as the winning entry in a name-the-hotel-contest. When the Monte Vista officially opened in January 1927, it was billed as the first full-service hotel in Arizona. It offered running water, flush toilets, telephones, and food service.

Thanks to a restoration project completed in 1986, guests today can relive the glamorous days of a bygone era as they sign in at the original front desk in the Western-style lobby and stroll down hallways past rooms bearing the names of famous guests. The hotel's 50 guest rooms vary in size and price, but all are comfortable and well appointed with antique reproductions, ceiling fans, and plush carpeting. The Zane Grey Suite is the hotel's largest, with the Humphrey Bogart Suite a close second. No doubt, the tribute to Bogart is due to his leading role in the award-winning classic *Casablanca*, which includes scenes filmed at the Monte Vista.

An old-fashioned coffee shop serving simple fare at reasonable prices is located just off the lobby. The Monte Vista Lounge, also adjacent to the lobby, is a popular showcase for regional talent who may someday make it big enough to get their names inscribed on rooms at the Monte Vista.

Rates

The 50 rooms and suites are available for $25 to $110. Meals are not included. Major credit cards are accepted.

Amenities

The rooms have telephones and cable television; some rooms share a shower. The hotel has a restaurant, gift shops, a hair salon, and an OTB/horse-racing lounge. It offers senior discounts and custom tours. The Monte Vista is convenient to restaurants, shops, and the train station.

Location

The hotel is in downtown Flagstaff at the corner of San Francisco Street and Aspen Avenue.

Inn at 410 Bed-and-Breakfast

Inn at 410 Bed-and-Breakfast

410 North Leroux Street
Flagstaff, Arizona 86001
phone: 800-774-2008 or 520-774-0088
Howard and Sally Krueger, owners/innkeepers

FLAGSTAFF'S ABUNDANCE OF FAST-FOOD eateries and look-alike motels makes it a convenient stop for travelers en route to the Grand Canyon but hardly an escape for those seeking a getaway from neon and noise. There are, however, wonderful romantic getaways in this pine-studded frontier town. One of the best is located two blocks from downtown in an area once known as "Nob Hill."

As its inclusion on the National Register of Historic Places affirms, the elegant Inn at 410 Bed-and-Breakfast is steeped in history. It was built in 1894 as a two-story farmhouse for prominent Flagstaff attorney Elias S. Clark, who later became Arizona's territorial attorney general. The contractor for the job was J. A. Wilson, a member of the party that erected the pine-sapling "flagstaff" for which the town is named.

In 1907, the home was sold to wealthy banker, rancher, and businessman Thomas Pollock to house his bride. Pollock brought in artisans from California to update the home to a Craftsman-style bungalow, the popular architectural style of the day. His bride, a teacher at Northern Arizona Normal School, which later became Northern Arizona University, undoubtedly was pleased with the added oak trim in the living and dining rooms, the tapered pillar at the entryway, the mahogany paneling, the built-in buffet, and the exterior corbels on the front porch. Stables and a carriage house were added at the back of the property, becoming part of the sprawling estate of the illustrious couple.

Following the death of Mrs. Pollock in 1941, the house was sold to a succession of owners. A fire in 1945 destroyed most of the second floor, and the upstairs was remodeled into apartments. Later, the stables were renovated and turned into offices. The property was eventually split, and a fraternity from Northern Arizona University moved into the house. In 1989, the home was purchased and opened as a bed-and-breakfast after an intensive two-year restoration project which produced a spacious new kitchen, a wheelchair-accessible guest room, and an innkeeper's residence on the second floor.

In 1993, current owners Sally and Howard Krueger fled their hectic Chicago lifestyle, moved to Flagstaff, and purchased the historic inn. Their appreciation for history and attention to detail are evident throughout the newly refurbished complex. The inviting wraparound front porch opens to a spacious parlor with polished oak trim, ceiling beams, and a flagstone fireplace. Each of the tastefully furnished guest rooms and suites provides a refreshing escape from the ordinary. The Southwest Suite is old Santa Fe, with a lodgepole-pine bed and a kiva fireplace. The Dakota Suite offers a dramatic red-and-black rustic cowboy decor, with bent-twig furniture and a stripped-log bed. Perhaps the most romantic room is the Victorian-style Tea Room, with its canopied bed, flowered wallpaper, and Jacuzzi for two.

Breakfast, a gourmet affair, is served in the sunny dining room or outdoors in the gazebo surrounded by flower gardens. The inn is a short walk from Flagstaff's historic district, where you can wander through buildings housing shops and cafes. When you return, the Kruegers will be waiting with iced tea and warm, freshly baked cookies.

Rates

The five guest rooms and four suites are available for $100 to $150. Breakfast and afternoon snacks are included. Well-behaved children are welcome, but pets are not. Visa and MasterCard are accepted.

Amenities

Some rooms have private entrances, fireplaces, and whirlpool tubs.

Location

The inn is just north of the downtown historic district. Follow Milton Road (which becomes Route 66 in downtown Flagstaff) to Leroux Street, then drive four and a half blocks north. The inn is on the right.

Briar Patch Inn

3190 North US 89A
Sedona, Arizona 86336
phone: 520-282-2342
fax: 520-282-2399
JoAnn and Ike Olson, innkeepers

DO YOU EVER DREAM OF ESCAPING to a secret place tucked back in the woods, where a creek ripples beside your cabin and deer and wild birds keep you company? If so, you can stop dreaming and experience the real thing at the Briar Patch Inn in Sedona.

Briar Patch Inn

The story of this forest hideaway began in 1876, when the area's first settlers, a family named Thompson, built their homestead along the bottom of Oak Creek Canyon, a place with a mild climate and fertile land. Indians once tended vegetables in the area, and wild blackberry vines covered the land. The old goat barn that now houses the office was built in the early 1880s.

The property changed hands several times before Ike and JoAnn Olson purchased the two-and-a-half-acre site in 1983. Three years later, they bought the adjoining six-acre parcel—formerly known as Rocky's Cabins—which included a collection of structures dating back to 1940. The rustic cabins, built for movie crews making Westerns in the Sedona area, featured Dutch doors, hand-hewn door handles, fireplaces, patios, and red-sandstone walkways. The cabins had since become a summer escape for Phoenicians seeking relief from the desert heat. Through the years, the Olsons, an environmentally conscious pair, have worked hard to retain the character of the cabins as they set about creating their magical wooded paradise.

The inn offers 16 log cabins nestled in a setting so lush, green, and serene that you'll feel time is standing still. You'll have a perfect opportunity to experience the beauty that draws people from throughout the world to the Sedona–Oak Creek Canyon area. Gravel paths and walkways flanked by leafy vines lead to charming cabins with ceiling beams, log walls, comfortable rustic furnishings, and private shaded patios. All have private baths, and most have fireplaces. Each cottage is artistically decorated to reflect Arizona's Native American and Mexican heritage.

The oldest cabin, Blue Jay, built in 1940 of stone and wood, features knotty pine walls, an aged brick fireplace, and a flagstone terrace. Sycamore Cabin has a rugged stone fireplace and lodge-pole furniture, while Acorn Cabin features a step-up bedroom, cozy shutters, and a floor-to-ceiling rock fireplace flanked by tree poles.

Breakfast, a heart-healthy affair of home-baked bread, crunchy granola, fresh fruit, and juice, can be enjoyed at tables in the main building, under the trees at a picnic table overlooking the creek, or in the privacy of your own patio. Refreshments and cookies are always available. During the summer months, breakfast is accompanied by the music of a violinist and a classical guitarist, who play beside the creek. On Sunday afternoons, chamber-music concerts are performed on the lawn. The inn offers occasional workshops in painting, Navajo weaving, Native American art, photography, music appreciation, and self-healing. A library and massages in your cottage are also available.

Rates

The 16 cottages range from $139 to $215. A full breakfast buffet is included. Visa, MasterCard, personal checks, and business checks are accepted. No pets are allowed. Smoking is not permitted in the cabins.

Amenities

The cottages have private baths, fireplaces, and shaded patios. Twelve units have kitchenettes. Masseuse service is available. A telephone is in the main building, and picnic tables are on the grounds.

Location

The inn is off US 89A three miles north of Sedona.

Forest Houses

Forest Houses
P.O. Box 250
9275 North US 89A
Oak Creek Canyon
Sedona, Arizona 86336
phone: 520-282-2999
Dave and Rhonda Peck, managers

THIS FOREST HIDEAWAY is for people who value the peace and privacy of natural surroundings far from the madding crowd. You'll find it tucked off the highway beside Oak Creek on 20 acres of heavily wooded land, where the sounds are those of the clear, cool mountain stream, the fish jumping, and the birds chattering in the lush sycamores, walnuts, and oaks.

The story of the Forest Houses began in 1930, when sculptor Robert Kittridge and his brother, accompanied by a pet monkey and a baby coyote, rode into Oak Creek Canyon on one of the first motorcycles built by Harley-Davidson. They bought the property for $60 an acre and began building their dream house, a log cabin that took them three years to complete.

A decade or so later, after World War II, Oak Creek Canyon became a favorite vacation area for the residents of booming Phoenix. Robert

Kittridge, who had apprenticed as a stone sculptor, stopped creating small sculptures and began constructing unique cottages, each designed to harmonize with the surroundings. His first rental house was a two-level rock structure. He completed five more houses during the 1950s. By 1960, he and his wife, Mary, were ready for a change. They purchased a 38-foot sailboat and—though they had never sailed before—embarked on a five-and-a-half-year around-the-world odyssey. After their return to Oak Creek Canyon, they created five more houses, the last in 1985. Although the Kittridges are now retired, the resort remains in the family. It is owned by Robert Kittridge, Jr., and operated by managers Dave and Rhonda Peck.

Each of the 12 cottages is an original design constructed of huge native boulders and log beams and offers fine views of Oak Creek, the canyon walls, and the surrounding forest. Some are located on a cliff above the creek, while others are tucked into the trees and the hillside. The cabins range in size from a cozy studio built on stilts with pines growing through the balconies to a spacious two-story with three bedrooms and four fireplaces. All have wood-burning stoves or fireplaces, patios or balconies, kitchens, and private baths.

Nature is the focus at this wooded retreat, where the favorite activities are trail walks, scenic hikes, bird-watching, wildlife observation, photography, trout fishing, and rest and relaxation. There are no telephones or televisions in the cabins to disturb the peace, although a public telephone is located on the grounds.

Rates

The 12 cabins are available for $85 to $120. Credit cards and personal checks are accepted. There is no charge for children under two years. Well-behaved pets are allowed. Check-in is at 3 P.M. and check-out at 11 A.M. The cabins are closed from New Year's Day until mid-March.

Garland's Oak Creek Lodge

P.O. Box 152
Sedona, Arizona 86339
phone: 520-282-3343
Gary and Mary Garland, owners/innkeepers

THE CLEAR, RIPPLING WATERS of Oak Creek wind below US 89A as you drive north from downtown Sedona, which can be a mob scene on weekends and holidays and during the summer. If the sounds and the sight of Oak Creek Canyon don't relax you sufficiently, the drive across the gently flowing stream to Garland's Oak Creek Lodge should do the trick.

The lodge sits on nine acres on the far side of the creek, surrounded by red canyon walls, towering oaks, and organic fruit orchards. Sixteen log cabins—some small, some large—are scattered about the grounds. Four of them are perched on a cliff above the rolling creek. All have porches and rustic, immaculate interiors with private baths, varnished wood floors, and old-fashioned hooked rugs. Most of the cabins have rugged river-rock fireplaces.

This lodge began as a homestead built in the early 1900s for an early settler named Jess Howard. Trees from the hills above the property were used to build the first log structure, which now serves as the lodge's

Garland's Oak Creek Lodge

kitchen. In the late 1920s, a family from Flagstaff, Frank and Catherine Todd and their son, Bill, purchased the property and began constructing cabins two by two. In time, Todd's Lodge became a sought-after getaway for locals and miners from Jerome, who came to fish and enjoy simple, delicious family-style meals. A main dining room was added in 1943—verified by the date on a buffalo nickel found under a cornerstone during a recent remodeling project.

In 1972, the Todds sold the lodge to a family from Phoenix, Bill and Georgiana Garland and their three children. The Garlands, longtime vacationers at Oak Creek, wanted to keep the "lodge" tradition alive. They added more cabins, updated the old ones, and planted organic vegetable gardens. The lodge's tradition of genuine hospitality and fine food continued—as did the loyal guests. So treasured are reservations at this serene retreat that most vacations are booked a year in advance. Some reservations reportedly have been contested in divorce cases.

The fact that there are no televisions, phones, or radios in the cabins adds to the lodge's tranquility. Life is laid-back and simple: fishing, hiking, reading a book, listening to the creek rush by, waiting for dinnertime at the rustic stone-and-wood dining room. The lodge's excellent cuisine has been featured in numerous national and regional publications. To keep stress at a minimum, the management removes decision making by serving a single dinner entrée, like Grilled Swordfish with Lemon and Herb Orzo or Roast Duck with Rhubarb Zinfandel Dressing, perhaps followed by fresh-from-the-orchard apple or peach pie.

Rates

The 16 cabins with private baths are available for $125 (single occupancy) to $185 (double occupancy); there is a $40 charge for each additional person in the cabin. A 15 percent service charge is added to all billings. Breakfast, tea with snacks, and dinner are included. The lodge is open from April 1 to November 15. Check-in is at 2 P.M. and check-out at noon.

Amenities

The cabins have fireplaces, and the lodge maintains a dining room. Guests can enjoy fishing in a trout-stocked stream, a hiking trail, a clay tennis court, a swimming hole, and ping pong and croquet facilities.

Location

The lodge is on US 89A eight miles north of Sedona and 20 miles south of Flagstaff. Turn west off the highway at the sign at Banjo Bill Campground, cross Oak Creek, and proceed to the lodge.

Lomacasi Cottages Bed-and-Breakfast

Lomacasi Cottages Bed-and-Breakfast
880 North US 89A
Sedona, Arizona 86336
phone: 800-521-3131 or 520-282-7912
fax: 520-282-2614

LOMACASI, A HOPI WORD meaning "place of happiness," is the perfect name for this eight-acre resort situated along the banks of Oak Creek amid towering red rocks. Nineteen secluded cottages with balconies offer a view of the clear, rippling waters of Oak Creek, a meandering creek which flows through Sedona from Arizona's highest mountains, the San Francisco Peaks in Flagstaff. Snugly tucked off the highway and hidden in the trees, Lomacasi is the ideal setting for those seeking a refreshing escape in a natural setting.

The Old Stonehouse, a historic red-rock cottage built in 1924, is the oldest structure at the resort. It is located on property acquired in the 1920s by Jess Purtyman, who traded his dry farm down the road for creek-side land. Purtyman hand-carved the floor joists for his house from juniper trees and used rocks from the creek for support and native flagstone for the exterior veneer, the fireplace, and the patio. Two more cottages were built on the property before it was sold in the 1940s. The new owner added a few more cabins to attract fishermen to the creek, which was stocked with trout on a weekly basis. The next owner, Nora Rose Walker, bought the property in the 1970s and turned the cabins into long-term rentals. She is best remembered for the rosebushes she collected during her travels around the country, which still bloom on the resort's beautifully landscaped grounds.

In 1996, Lomacasi was acquired by ILX, Inc., owner of the elegant Los Abrigados Resort and Spa, located a mile away. This distinguished resort serves as an alternate breakfast location for Lomacasi guests, who are also welcome to use the health spa, restaurants, and gift shops at Los Abrigados.

Most of the cottages face the creek, which is bordered by picnic gazebos and gardens. At one end of the property is a playground with facilities for bocce ball, horseshoes, and badminton. At the other end are the Naamati Gardens, a picturesque setting used for weddings and other special occasions. Fruit trees, maples, and sycamores provide a leafy canopy above gravel pathways that wind between cottages with names like Daydream and Morningstar. The studio, one-bedroom, and two-bedroom units feature comfortable furnishings and interesting old photographs dating to the turn of the century. Some cottages have ceiling beams, brick or rock fireplaces, and hammocks for creek-side viewing. The units nearest the creek are attached, while freestanding cottages offer a hidden-in-the-forest setting. All provide a glorious escape from high-tech life.

Rates

The 19 cottages (studio, one-bedroom, and two-bedroom) are available for $95 to $195. Children 15 and under may stay with parents at no additional charge; there is a $10 surcharge for each additional person. Daily coffee and continental breakfast are included. Credit cards are accepted. No pets are allowed.

Saddle Rock Ranch

P.O. Box 10095
255 Rock Ridge Drive
Sedona, Arizona 86336
phone: 520-282-7640
fax: 520-282-6829
Fran and Dan Bruno, innkeepers

THE STUNNING RED ROCKS of Sedona have lured moviemakers and
photographers for more than half a century. Numerous Western films
have been made in this rugged, sun-splashed land. Zane Grey's *Call of the
Canyon* and other memorable cowboy flicks—*Angel and the Badman, Broken Arrow*, and *The Texas Trail*—were filmed at Saddle Rock Ranch. Some
of Hollywood's greatest screen cowboys—Hopalong Cassidy, Jimmy
Stewart, John Wayne, and Randolph Scott—spent time here. Lest visitors forget, a 1907 covered wagon at the bottom of the private, winding,
tree-lined drive serves as a reminder of the ranch's former role.

Saddle Rock began in the 1920s as a 6,000-acre horse ranch which
spread across a hillside overlooking red-rock vistas. The main lodge, a
sandstone-and-adobe structure with massive beam ceilings and floors made
of wood and flagstones, was constructed in 1926. The ranch served as a
movie estate, dude ranch, and Western retreat through the mid-1950s

Saddle Rock Ranch

and later became a summer residence for Senator Barry Goldwater's family. In 1988, the trimmed-down three-acre ranch was opened as a bed-and-breakfast by new owners Fran and Dan Bruno, former managers with the Ritz Carlton hotels in California.

Thanks to a sweeping, 17-mile-wide view of Sedona's breathtaking landscape, the Old West has never been more romantic than at this elegant historic getaway. The spacious, comfortably furnished parlor features huge windows and fine antiques, including an 1850s pump organ in perfect working condition. Though electric lighting has replaced the original gaslights and air conditioning and heating have been added for guest comfort, the historic flavor of the house remains. Guests will not be surprised to learn that Saddle Rock is soon to be listed on the National Register of Historic Places.

Each of the inn's three well-appointed guest suites has a wood-burning rock fireplace, a private bath, and inviting views. From the Saddle Rock Suite, you can see the scenic valley, and from the Rose Garden Room, a blooming terraced hillside. The Honeymoon Cottage, up the hill, is a former cowboy bunkhouse and artist's studio. Romantic gourmet breakfasts featuring such items as blue-corn heart-shaped waffles are served in the main lodge's cheerful breakfast room or on the deck beside the pool.

An added attraction is the day-long journeys led by Dan Bruno to the Second and First Mesas of the Hopi Nation, where guests can observe authentic Native American pottery and baskets being handcrafted by Hopi masters. For those who'd rather remain at the ranch, an exquisite collection of native Zuni, Navajo, and Hopi jewelry, colorful kachina dolls, and other authentic handmade crafts is on display in the parlor.

Rates

The three suites with private baths are available for $120 to $140 per night. A two-night minimum stay is required during low season and a four-night minimum during high season, which runs from late March through early June and from late September through early November. Ask about special rates. Children over age 13 are welcome. Breakfast, refreshments, and afternoon snacks are included. Smoking and pets are not allowed. Traveler's checks and personal checks are accepted, but credit cards are not.

Amenities

The ranch provides full concierge service, terry robes, pool towels, a pool, a spa, a house phone, and television.

Location

From US 89A, turn south onto Airport Road and drive 0.1 mile to Chimney Spire. Turn right, proceed to Valley View, and turn right again. At the first fork in the road, turn left onto Saddle Rock Circle. Turn left onto Rock Ridge Drive and follow it to another fork; turn right and look for the Saddle Rock Ranch sign. Follow the driveway to the top of the hill.

CENTRAL ARIZONA

Jerome, Prescott, White Mountains,
Wickenburg, Litchfield Park, Scottsdale,
Paradise Valley, Phoenix, Mesa,
Globe, Chandler

IN THE CENTRAL PORTION of the state, mountain ranges meet arid deserts, and the landscape is dotted with both large and tiny towns. There's also a sprinkling of abandoned ghost towns, leftovers of Arizona's mining days. The rush for gold, silver, and copper began in such places as **Prescott**, the first capital of the Arizona Territory; **Jerome**, a sturdy survivor clinging to the side of Cleopatra Hill; and **Globe**, tucked in a narrow valley in the Apache Mountains.

Once known as "the Wickedest Town in the West," Jerome has survived not only devastating fires—which blasted from the underground mines and shook the town's structures right off their foundations—but abandonment and ghost-town status after the mines closed in the 1950s. Resurrected by artists and writers in the 1970s, Jerome has found a new role as a tourist attraction, its sloping streets peopled by visitors wandering into and out of historic buildings that house colorful galleries and shops.

Prescott, often called "the West's Most Eastern Town," charms visitors with streets lined with late-19th-century buildings and regal Victorian residences. Over 400 local structures claim a listing on the National Register of Historic Places. Centered around pleasant Courthouse Plaza and the 1916 Yavapai County Courthouse, the town has a Midwestern heritage and a small-town flavor. Sitting about a mile above sea level, Prescott has long been a favorite summer escape for Valley of the Sun residents seeking relief from the desert heat.

To the east are the White Mountains, whose altitudes range from 7,000 to 11,000 feet. The mountains offer a cool, forested retreat during summer and skiing during winter at Sunrise Park Resort, owned and operated by the White Mountains Apache tribe.

The twin towns of **Lakeside** and **Pinetop** have names that reflect their beautiful surroundings.

The tiny hamlet of **Greer**, founded by Mormon pioneers in 1879, is a fisherman's delight, thanks to the three surrounding Greer Lakes and the Little Colorado River, which runs right through the town.

By the time you reach sleepy **Alpine** in the far eastern section of the state, you may have to remind yourself that you are still in Arizona and not in some Swiss mountain village.

Dude ranches began to spring up around the state in the 1920s and 1930s. **Wickenburg**, northwest of Phoenix, once had so many that it claimed to be "the Dude Ranch Capital of the World." There's still a sense of the Old West in this laid-back town, where Henry Wickenburg struck it rich at the Vulture Mine in 1863. The town is surrounded by rocky hills, and its downtown streets are lined with Western-style buildings.

Along with copper and cattle, Arizona relied on the production of cotton and citrus. In 1916, the Goodyear Tire Company began sowing cotton seeds along the Agua Fria River for use in making a heavy-duty tire designed by Paul Litchfield. Arizona's climate proved ideal for growing long-staple cotton, resulting in a cotton-farming venture that transformed the desert into a 38,000-acre landscaped empire named **Litchfield Park**. The adobe structure which once provided lodging for Goodyear executives developed through the years into the historic, world-class Wigwam Resort.

Mountains ring the 1,000-square-mile valley formed by the Salt River. Commonly referred to as "the Valley of the Sun" for its lack of rainfall, it includes Arizona's capital, **Phoenix**, and the cities that have grown around it, including **Scottsdale, Mesa**, and **Chandler**. The valley was first farmed by ancient Hohokam Indians, who designed a canal system they later abandoned in the mid-1400s. In 1867, the canals were revived due to the foresight of a former Confederate army officer named Jack Swilling. By 1870, a town site was laid out for Phoenix, a city destined to rise from the ashes of a vanished civilization. By the time Arizona achieved statehood in 1912, irrigation efforts had expanded thanks to the newly constructed Roosevelt Dam and the Salt River Project. The Phoenix area was becoming known as a desert oasis.

By the 1930s, resorts were catering to Easterners looking for relief from frozen winter temperatures. They found sunny playgrounds at the San Marcos Resort in Chandler, the first Arizona resort to offer a 100-acre golf course, tennis, polo, horseback riding, and a constant flow of social activities. When the San Carlos Hotel, the first high-rise in Phoenix, opened in 1928, it was touted as one of the Southwest's most modern hotels, offering circulating ice water, air conditioning, and elevators. The 1930s and 1940s marked the opening of glittering resorts like the Arizona Biltmore, the Royal Palms Inn in northern Phoenix, and the Camelback Inn in Scottsdale. Today, metropolitan Phoenix is one of the fastest-growing areas in the country, its population topping 2 million.

Things to do and see

PRESCOTT AREA

Sharlot Hall Museum. This excellent three-acre museum features a dozen structures, including the two-story Governor's Mansion, built of logs on the site in 1864. For information, call 520-445-3122.

Montezuma Castle National Monument. These well-preserved ruins of a five-story stone-and-mortar structure built by Sinagua Indians in the 12th and 13th centuries are tucked under a cliff 100 feet above Beaver Creek. The monument is located off Interstate 17 between Camp Verde and McGuireville. For information, call 520-567-3322.

SCOTTSDALE

Old Town Scottsdale. Rustic storefronts and wooden sidewalks bring back the flavor of the Old West in shops lining Main and Brown Streets.

PHOENIX

Desert Botanical Garden. The answers to everything you've ever wanted to know about the desert plants of Arizona can be found along a 1.5-mile trail that winds past more than 2,000 species of cacti and other exotic blooms. The garden is located off Galvin Parkway in Pagago Park. For information, call 602-941-1217.

Heard Museum. This museum houses one of the best exhibits on Indians of the Southwest you'll find anywhere. It is located in a Spanish Colonial home on East Monte Vista Road. Call 602-252-8848 for tour times.

Heritage Square. This block of renovated turn-of-the-century houses in downtown Phoenix is dominated by the 1895 Rosson House, a gingerbread-trimmed Victorian. Call 602-262-5071 for tour times.

WICKENBURG

Desert Caballeros Western Museum. Discover the Old West in this 20,000-square-foot museum, which includes a large art gallery. It is located downtown at 21 North Frontier Street. For information, call 602-684-7075.

Ghost City Inn Bed-and-Breakfast

Ghost City Inn Bed-and-Breakfast

P.O. Box 382
541 North Main Street
Jerome, Arizona 86331
phone/fax: 520-63GHOST

AT THE BEGINNING of the 20th century, the copper-mining town of Jerome was the talk of the territory. With 88 miles of underground tunnels, a population of 15,000, and sloping streets lined with noisy saloons, gambling halls, and bordellos, it was known as "the Wickedest Town in the West." No doubt, if the walls at the Ghost City Inn Bed-and-Breakfast could talk, we'd hear some colorful tales of Jerome's rip-roaring boomtown days.

Ghosts are said to inhabit this white, two-story frame structure trimmed in brown, built in 1898 as a boardinghouse for copper miners. Like the town itself, the sturdy building managed to survive the destructive fires that raged through the streets and the dynamiting disasters that caused some of the town's buildings to slip down the slopes. Perhaps the spirits are those of old miners reluctant to leave their boardinghouse. Chances are they never had it so good as guests do today at the handsomely restored structure, which was reopened in 1994.

The inn has a red tin roof and two broad verandas that stretch across the entire front of the house. Inside on the main level, the original hardwood floors and woodwork complement the turn-of-the-century Victorian decor. Five of the inn's six rooms are on the second floor. All are beautifully decorated with period furnishings, most in the Victorian style. Some rooms open onto the spacious verandas, which offer a breathtaking view of the Verde Valley and the terraced red rocks of Sedona. The "Ladies of the Night Room," with its antique brass bed, is said to have housed some of Jerome's famous madams, like the Cuban Queen, Miss Jennie Banters, and Madam Pearl. There are cozy sitting areas upstairs and down, and a delightful, sunny patio is in the small courtyard off the parlor.

Today, life is pretty quiet in Jerome except on weekends, when hordes of tourists fill the sidewalks and wander into and out of the old buildings lining the steep and winding streets. A stay at this quaint inn offers a restful, serene escape from hectic modern life. Guests are treated to a royal dose of pampering that includes a gourmet breakfast, afternoon tea, evening turn-down service with chocolates on the pillows, and comfy blue terry-cloth robes to snuggle into after a relaxing bath.

Rates

The six rooms are available for $65 to $85. Breakfast is included. Smoking is not permitted indoors. No pets are allowed. Checks, cash, Visa, MasterCard, and Discover are accepted.

Amenities

Four rooms have private baths, and two share a bath. A television, a phone, and a fax are located in common areas. The inn has verandas and a courtyard and offers afternoon tea and turn-down service.

Location

The inn is on Main Street (US 89A).

Inn at Jerome

P.O. Box 901
309 Main Street
Jerome, Arizona 86331
phone: 800-634-5094 or 520-634-5094

BIG-TIME MINING OPERATIONS began in Jerome in 1883, when it was discovered the town sat above a vast deposit of copper. Soon, blast furnaces appeared on the scene. Later, a narrow-gauge railroad was built. In the years that followed, billions of dollars' worth of copper were produced from more than 88 miles of underground tunnels. The booming and blasting continued for over 70 years, attracting so many saloons, gambling halls, and bordellos that Jerome earned a reputation as a wild and wicked town. Many of the businesses were little more than hastily put-together tent operations. Fires devastated the clapboard town three times before 1900, but each time, Jerome rebuilt.

The structure that houses the Inn at Jerome was erected after a fire raged through town in 1899. J. H. Clinkscale, a local insurance adjuster, wanted a building as fireproof as possible, so he built his two-story structure of poured, reinforced concrete, its walls 18 inches thick in places. The sturdy structure, which originally housed a hardware store on the lower level and offices upstairs, still bears the builder's name across the top. Other operations including a mortuary and a hotel occupied the structure throughout the years. Thanks to its solid construction, the building easily withstood the endless dynamite blasting that caused a row of businesses across the street to slide down the slope.

When the mines finally closed in 1953, the former boom town became a ghost town. Some structures were moved down the hill to other towns, while others like the Clinkscale Building were abandoned as the population dwindled to a mere 50 inhabitants.

The forgotten town was rescued from oblivion when counterculture pioneers of the 1960s and 1970s moved in and began renovating homes and opening shops. Now, Jerome is a mecca for travelers wanting to turn back the clock and meander through the quaint shops and cafes which line the narrow, sloping streets. Many book a room in the Inn at Jerome, right in the center of town.

Reminiscent of a quaint European hotel, the inn is located on the second floor of the building, above the first-floor restaurant and full-service bar. At the top of the stairs, a Victorian parlor with a cozy fireplace and antique furnishings offers guests a pleasant place for quiet conversation and complimentary morning coffee. Eight handsomely furnished guest rooms with antiques from around the world have been decorated according to different themes. Little Daisy, named for Jerome's most famous mine, has a French oak bed and a view of the entire Verde Valley all the way to Flagstaff. Another room features cowboy memorabilia and a step-up four-poster bed handcrafted by local artists. The Honeymoon Getaway features an antique spool bed and views of old Jerome.

Rates

The inn's eight rooms range in price from $55 to $85. No pets are allowed. Major credit cards are accepted.

Amenities

Two rooms have private baths, and the others share a bath with one other room. The inn has pedestal sinks in all rooms, color televisions, terry robes, ceiling fans, and air conditioning. A restaurant and full-service bar are downstairs.

Location

The inn is on Main Street near First Avenue, next to the town hall.

Jerome Grand Hotel

Jerome Grand Hotel

P.O. Box 757
200 Hill Street
Jerome, Arizona 86331
phone: 520-634-8200
fax: 520-639-0299
Bob and Debra Altherr, managers

THE REWARD FOR MAKING the winding four-mile drive up Mingus Mountain to Jerome is the spectacular view of the Verde Valley. At an elevation of 5,400 feet, and with town limits that vary 1,500 feet from the highest to the lowest points, Jerome offers breathtaking vistas from just about anywhere in town. But for the ultimate panoramic sweep of the Verde Valley, which includes the red rocks of Sedona and the San Francisco Peaks beyond Flagstaff, ask for a balcony room at the Jerome Grand Hotel. Sitting on a ledge above town, the hotel boasts the highest historic accommodations in the entire Verde Valley.

This enormous reinforced-concrete structure was designed and built in 1926 by the United Verde Copper Company to serve as a hospital for Jerome and the surrounding communities. When it opened, the United Verde Hospital was one of the most modern hospitals in the West. The building was constructed with three stories above a ground/basement level, but another story which included a balcony was added in 1929. In 1951, when mining operations ceased and Jerome was becoming a ghost town, the hospital was closed and kept in standby condition, ready to reopen if needed. The need never arose, and the building was converted into apartments in the 1970s.

In 1994, the Phelps Dodge Mining Company finally sold the old hospital to a couple of preservation-minded buyers, who pledged to renovate the 30,000-square-foot structure. After two years of hard work, the refurbished structure was reopened as Van-Alan's Jerome Grand Hotel.

The hotel's main entrance, located in the former hospital's emergency area, opens to a pleasant reception area. Interesting leftovers from the building's original role—drawers, mailboxes, card holders, and X-ray file boxes—have been put to use behind the counter. The old Otis elevator, wide enough to accommodate patients in gurneys, now transports hotel guests to their rooms. The original Kewanee boiler system continues to heat the building today. The structure's role as a hospital is reflected in the wide corridors, the transoms over the doors, and the patient call lights—elaborate items for the time. The original fixtures, high ceilings, and floor tiles remain, but the guest rooms have been updated with private baths and antique furnishings. French doors and lace curtains soften the institutional atmosphere of the former hospital wards.

The top-of-the-world views that set this historic hotel apart are best enjoyed from the balcony on the fourth floor. The wrought-iron railing, which was raised in the early 1930s after a patient's fatal jump, has now been lowered to allow guests unobstructed viewing.

The recently renovated lounge and dining room on the second level occupy former doctors' offices. The walls were removed to create an open, spacious room with elegant arched windows overlooking the valley. Furnished in the style of the 1920s, the inviting room features an **L**-shaped oak bar with brass railings, antique furnishings, and a dance floor with a bandstand. It's a perfect place to celebrate this historic structure's rebirth as the only full-service hotel to appear in Jerome in more than 40 years.

Rates

The 32 rooms are available for $55 to $85. Most major credit cards are accepted. Check-in is at 3 P.M. and check-out at noon. No pets are allowed.

Amenities

The rooms have private baths. A restaurant, a lounge, and a gift shop are on the premises. The hotel is within walking distance of downtown Jerome's attractions.

Location

The hotel is two blocks above downtown Jerome. Follow US 89A to Hill Street. Turn onto Hill Street and follow it to the top of the hill. Turn left to the hotel's parking area.

The Surgeon's House Bed-and-Breakfast

The Surgeon's House Bed-and-Breakfast

P.O. Box 998
101 Hill Street
Jerome, Arizona 86331
phone: 800-639-1452 or 520-639-1452
Andrea Prince, owner/innkeeper

"DRIVE UP THE HILL AND INTO THE PAST" is the slogan at The Surgeon's House, an elegant, white two-story Spanish-style structure perched on a hillside 5,200 feet in elevation. The slogan accurately describes the feeling most travelers experience when they arrive in the old mining town of Jerome, which looks much as it did nearly a century ago.

The spacious mansion was built in 1917 by the United Verde Copper Company as a residence for the chief surgeon at the company's hospital, located next door. The 2,300-square-foot home, with its luxurious interior and commanding view of downtown Jerome and the expansive Verde Valley, apparently was not enough to soothe the troubles of the first chief surgeon, Dr. L. P. Kaull, who committed suicide in 1923 by self-administering a lethal drug.

The next chief surgeon was Dr. Arthur Carlson, who moved into the home with his wife, Maude. The Carlsons enjoyed an active social life and entertained guests frequently at their elegant mansion. Carlson was active in civic and political activities, serving as mayor and as a councilman for three terms. He remained chief surgeon until 1945, when he moved off Mingus Mountain to Cottonwood to start a hospital.

Jerome's hospital closed in 1951, mining operations ceased a few years later, and the former surgeon's house became a rental residence. Owners came and went. In 1992, the home was purchased by Andrea Prince, an engineering consultant looking for a stress-free life. She spent four months working with local artisans before opening her elegant residence as The Surgeon's House Bed-and-Breakfast.

The expansive windows, which range from a nine-foot-wide picture window in the living and dining room to floor-to-ceiling arched windows in the atrium, allow breathtaking views of the town and valley. The high ceilings, the oak floors, and the furniture upholstered in restful taupe and white add to the home's bright, open feeling and create a good backdrop for the owner's interesting collection of antiques and memorabilia. For bold color, step into the kitchen, where Prince prepares her lavish morning meals on an old commercial stove amidst bright turquoise walls and a black-and-white-checked ceramic-tile floor.

Three guest rooms (or two guest suites) and two full baths are located beyond the colorful stained-glass window at the top of the stairs. The cheery Master Suite features a private balcony overlooking the valley and the gardens below and a private sitting room with a "fainting couch" once used in a Jerome brothel. The spacious Blue Room has an old-fashioned iron bed frame, deep blue walls, and a valley view. The former maid's room has Mennonite furniture. Behind the main house in the former chauffeur's quarters, the intimate Queen Suite offers a private bath, a kitchenette, and a secluded patio.

Breakfast, which often consists of numerous courses, is designed to carry you through until dinnertime. You may dine in the lovely dining room or out on the garden patio in the morning sun, surrounded by terraced flower beds and sweeping views of the Verde Valley.

Rates

The suite with shared bath, the suite with private bath and balcony, and the detached suite with queen bed, private bath, kitchenette, and patio are available for $90 to $125 (double occupancy). Full breakfast, snacks, and beverages are included. Visa, MasterCard, and American Express are accepted. Supervised children are welcome, but pets are not.

Amenities

A television, a radio, and an alarm clock are in each room. The Surgeon's House offers a living room, a dining room, a kitchen, an atrium, porches, yards, gardens, a hot tub, an in-house masseur, and a fireplace.

Location

The Surgeon's House sits approximately a block and a half above Main Street (US 89A). Follow Main Street to Clark Street. Follow Clark Street to Hill Street, a narrow cobblestone lane near the Episcopal church / Jerome Historical Society office. Follow Hill Street and look for the inn on the right. Private, off-street parking is in front of the garage.

Hassayampa Inn

Hassayampa Inn
**122 East Gurley Street
Prescott, Arizona 86301
phone: 800-322-1927 or 520-778-9434
Bill and Georgia Teich, owners**

SOME OF THE OLDEST and best-preserved examples of 19th-century American architecture in the Southwest are in Prescott, the state's first territorial capital, founded in 1864. More than a century later, the town's character clearly shows the Midwestern and Eastern roots of its early residents, who were determined to resist the Pueblo Revival style when designing their town. The four-story Hassayampa Inn, built in 1927 and named after a nearby river, is a perfect example of their resistance.

The story of the inn began in the 1920s, when residents of Prescott made the bold decision to erect a hotel to attract summer tourists from Phoenix who were seeking to escape the desert's unbearable heat. Money was raised through public subscription for a grand hotel to be erected near the picturesque Courthouse Plaza. It was to be designed by the Southwest's most distinguished architect, Henry Trost of El Paso, Texas. However, Trost's Pueblo-style design didn't suit the townspeople, mostly Midwestern in origin, who preferred brick over adobe. The result was a muted Spanish Colonial Revival exterior of red brick trimmed in crisp white, with a bell tower.

Inside the inn's lobby, however, it's obvious that the Midwestern design was compromised for the sake of a handsome territorial ambiance. Ornate ceiling artwork and embossed copper panels combine with arched windows and a tiled fireplace to create one of Arizona's most comfortable and colorful "Old World" lobbies. Tastefully decorated, the spacious room would suit anyone from a wealthy landowner to a silent-screen cowboy like Tom Mix, who spent considerable time at the inn when in town filming Westerns.

Like a number of other important Prescott structures, the Hassayampa Inn suffered through a period of neglect during the 1960s and 1970s. It later underwent a restoration so thorough that it bankrupted the owners. Rescue came in 1990, when current owners Bill and Georgia Teich returned the Hassayampa to its status as grande dame of downtown Prescott, more glamorous today than it was in its prime.

Soft classical music drifts through the lobby, which gleams with glazed tile, a grand piano, and elegant tapestry chairs. The original elevator is still in operation at the rear of the lobby. All guest rooms have been updated with private baths and wall-to-wall carpeting and are attractively furnished, some with original 1927 pieces and commissioned watercolors of Prescott's Victorian buildings.

Guests are invited to begin their day with a complimentary breakfast selected from the menu of the elegant Peacock Dining Room, located off the inn's lobby. The inn's friendly, professional staff is always ready to help arrange tours or dinner reservations. Located in the heart of downtown Prescott, the hotel is steps away from the town's many antique stores, gift shops, and restaurants. A block away on Whiskey Row, a saloon or two is still in operation to remind visitors of the street's notorious past.

Rates

The 58 rooms and 10 suites are available for $89 to $175. Breakfast is included. No pets are allowed. Credit cards are accepted.

Amenities

Televisions and phones are in the rooms. The inn offers a restaurant, a lounge, a lobby, a courtyard, bellman service, and private parking.

Location

The Hassayampa is in downtown Prescott at the corner of Gurley Street and Marina Avenue.

Hotel St. Michael

205 West Gurley Street
Prescott, Arizona 86301
phone: 800-678-3757 or 520-776-1999
fax: 520-776-7318

The enormous fired-brick Hotel St. Michael was built in 1901 over the ashes of the three-story Hotel Burke. No matter that the Hotel Burke, built in 1891, had been advertised as "the only absolutely fireproof building in Prescott." It burned to the ground like the rest of Whiskey Row in a fire that destroyed the town's entire business district. It's interesting to note that on that fateful night, the fires didn't put a stop to business on

Hotel St. Michael

Whiskey Row. The crowds simply moved across the street to the plaza and continued to party.

The new, larger hotel, designed in the Second Renaissance Revival style by a prominent Phoenix firm, featured a stone basement, fired-brick upper floors, and gargoyles under the roofline. Renamed the Hotel St. Michael in 1907, it boasted more than 50,000 square feet of space, 110 rooms, and an assortment of shops. The grand hotel quickly became a social center for locals and visiting dignitaries and celebrities like Teddy Roosevelt, Wyatt Earp, Will Rogers, Tom Mix, and Sun Yat-sen, the first president of China.

The hotel was operated by one of the original partners, John Duke, and his daughter, Mamie, until the mid-1940s. The succession of owners that followed included a "Miss Charlene," whose penchant for rosy interiors was responsible for the splashes of pink that still remain on the walls in the basement, once the site of the hotel's shoeshine operation, barbershop, and bar. The basement is also the location of underground tunnels rumored to have once provided a convenient passageway to the courthouse, located across the street.

Through the years, remodeling efforts destroyed much of the hotel's historic character. For a few years in the 1980s, the St. Michael stood empty. In 1988, the building was purchased by the current owners, who began the challenging process of returning the St. Michael to its turn-of-the-century splendor. The original pressed-metal ceilings were uncovered, the hardwood floors refinished, and the wavy windows of handmade glass repaired. The elevator, installed in 1920, was put back into service; Prescott's first, it ranks today as the oldest working elevator in this part of Arizona.

The accommodations have been pared to 72 rooms. All have private baths, high ceilings, and Victorian decor that reflects the Old West. The well-appointed rooms feature delicate floral wallcoverings, wainscoting, and antique furnishings. History blends easily with the modern conveniences we've come to expect: telephones, color television, and air conditioning.

The downstairs lobby opens to a collection of specialty shops called St. Michael's Alley. At the corner of the building is a charming coffee shop. From a seat in the window, you can sip cappuccino and watch the world go by on the sidewalks and on the pathways in Courthouse Plaza, across the street.

Rates

The double, queen, king, and family units and suites are available for $36 to $72. All have private baths. Continental breakfast is included.

Amenities

Each guest room has cable television and a direct-dial telephone. A bar, a coffee shop, and specialty shops are in the lobby.

Location

The hotel is on the corner of Montezuma and Gurley Streets in downtown Prescott.

Hotel Vendome

Hotel Vendome

230 South Cortez Street
Prescott, Arizona 86303
phone: 520-776-0900
Rama and Amrish Patel, innkeepers

THE HOTEL VENDOME, a broad, two-story red-brick structure with wide verandas on both levels, is a storyteller's dream. Built in 1917 by a lucky miner who struck it rich, the building was scheduled to open as a dignified hotel. But according to the story, the owner was jilted by his ladylove shortly after the completion of the building, and the dejected suitor covered up the fancy wainscoting and opened the place as a boardinghouse for miners.

Eventually, the structure assumed its intended role as a hotel, providing residence for tuberculosis sufferers who came to Prescott in the 1920s to recuperate in the clean mountain air. There's a story that the ghost of Abby Byers, a tuberculosis victim who died in the hotel in 1921, still makes mischief in her old room. The Vendome was also a favorite of screen cowboys filming Western movies in the area during the 1930s.

Through the years, various owners came and went. By the 1960s, the hotel had fallen into a sorry state of neglect. When a group of preservation-minded investors rescued it in 1983, plaster was falling from the walls, layers of paint covered the original woodwork, and the lobby had been emptied of its original furnishings. During the ambitious restoration project that followed, the wainscoting was carefully uncovered and refinished and the original front desk and signal board—which enabled guests to contact the front desk in the days before telephones—were rounded up and returned to the lobby.

Because the Vendome's interior and exterior are essentially unchanged, a feeling of timelessness pervades the old hotel. There's a sense of being transported back to the Prescott of the early 1900s. The 21 spacious guests rooms are bright, uncluttered, and furnished with handsome period reproductions and wallpaper. All the rooms have private baths; many have the original claw-foot tubs and pull-chain commodes, and some have sunken garden tubs. Photos and newspaper articles from Prescott's early days line the walls of the first- and second-floor hallways and the downstairs lobby. The wide verandas stretching across the entire front of the structure provide an excellent opportunity to sit back and watch the world go by. Courthouse Plaza, Whiskey Row, and Prescott's downtown shops and restaurants are only a block or two away.

Continental breakfast is served in the lobby on the cherry-wood counter, which doubles as a beer-and-wine bar. Owners Rama and Amrish Patel, who purchased the hotel in 1994 as a Clarion Carriage House Inn, enjoy providing their guests with a romantic Old World escape from everyday life and a chance, perhaps, to create a story of their own.

Rates

Rooms rent for $79 to $159. Continental breakfast is included. Children are welcome, but pets are discouraged.

Amenities

Twin- and queen-size beds and two-room suites are available. The rooms have private baths, telephones, and color television. A wine bar is in the lobby. Limited room service is available.

Location

The hotel is on South Cortez Street between Goodwin and Carleton Streets, a half-block south of Courthouse Plaza and the center of downtown Prescott.

The Marks House

203 East Union Street
Prescott, Arizona 86303
phone: 800-370-MARK or 520-778-4632
Dottie and Harold Viehweg, innkeepers

THE ROMANTIC CHARM of old Prescott lies in its preserved turn-of-the-century structures, including the many handsomely restored Victorian residences along the tree-lined streets near the heart of town. One of the most elegant is The Marks House, a yellow, turreted Queen Anne standing proudly on a sloped corner overlooking Courthouse Plaza.

It took two years for wealthy wholesale liquor distributor, community leader, and former mayor Jake Marks to complete the two-story, 11-room

The Marks House

mansion. The house, which occupies two city lots, was built in stages as materials ordered from a catalog arrived at the train depot a few blocks away. Sparing no expense, Marks imported redwood from California and hired master craftsmen to build the veranda, to install ornately carved copper door hinges and plates, and to put a parquet floor in the dining room. Completed in 1894, it was the first home in what became known as the "Nob Hill" area.

After Jake Marks and his wife, Josephine, died in the early 1900s, their former residence was converted into apartments. It later became a rest home for the elderly. In 1980, restoration began to return the old mansion to its original role as an elegant single-family residence. In 1987, the carefully restored structure was opened as a bed-and-breakfast. Current innkeepers Dottie and Harold Viehweg assumed operation of the Marks House in 1991, when it was purchased by their daughter, Beth Maitland, an actress in the CBS daytime drama *The Young and the Restless*.

The undisputed star at the Marks House is the luxurious Queen Anne Suite, which features a private bath with a claw-foot tub and a sitting room in a circular turret, from which guests can enjoy a view stretching from the heart of downtown to Thumb Butte in the distance. Two additional suites, the cheerful Tea Rose and elegant Princess Victoria, also share the inn's upper level. The largest guest room, the Ivy Suite, is downstairs on the main level; it features two adjoining rooms with tiger-oak antiques, book-filled shelves, and a private bath with an antique vanity.

The decor throughout the house reflects the Victorian era, the favorite style of the original owners. The walls are painted in colors matching those used during Victorian times, and the antique furnishings in the bay-windowed parlor date to the late 1800s. Even the white picket fence is identical to the one that framed the house a century ago. The inviting veranda that sweeps around the side of the house allows views of Courthouse Plaza, the distant mountains, and spectacular sunsets.

Listed on the National Register of Historic Places, the inn is reportedly haunted by two ghosts that occasionally thump and bump in the night. One is said to be a harmless prankster, the other a mother searching for a lost child. Perhaps they are reluctant to leave the inviting atmosphere and the appetizing aromas that drift through the spacious dining room, where Dottie serves family-style breakfasts prepared from recipes published in *The Marks House Cookbook*.

Rates

The three one-room suites and the two-bedroom suite are available for $75 to $135. A full breakfast and afternoon hors d'oeuvres are included. No pets are allowed. Smoking is not permitted indoors. Credit cards are accepted.

Amenities

The rooms have private baths, feather beds, and antiques. A television and a telephone are in common areas. A small gift shop is on the premises. The house is within walking distance of downtown shops and restaurants.

Location

The inn is at the corner of Marina and Union Streets in historic downtown Prescott.

Mount Vernon Inn

204 North Mount Vernon Avenue
Prescott, Arizona 86301
phone: 520-778-0886
web site: http://prescottlink.com/mtvrnon/index.htm
e-mail: mtvrnon@primenet.com
Michele and Jerry Neumann, innkeepers

PRESCOTT, ESTABLISHED IN 1864, is one of Arizona's oldest and most picturesque towns. The pleasant downtown Courthouse Plaza, surrounded by handsomely restored century-old structures, sends out an irresistible invitation to passersby to turn back the clock and slow down. It's not

Mount Vernon Inn

surprising that the town is a favorite getaway for Phoenicians, who have been escaping to Prescott since the invention of the automobile to savor its unhurried, small-town appeal and mile-high summer temperatures.

It's easy to forget the high-tech life in this town, where history is celebrated and Victorian architecture revered. Prescott is an open-air museum of Arizona's finest Victorian structures, many of them located on Mount Vernon Avenue a few blocks up the hill from the center of town. This broad boulevard is lined with stately mansions begging for attention with their gingerbread trim and whimsical turrets.

Among these storybook places is the Mount Vernon Inn. This two-story frame structure, painted a deep gray and trimmed in white, stands proudly among shade trees on a quiet corner in the center of the Mount Vernon Historical District. It features a distinctive "candle-snuffer" turret, gables, pediments, and a columned porch that wraps around a portion of the front and side. A wrought-iron fence frames the house and gardens, adding the proper finishing touch to a prim Victorian portrait.

The elegant residence was built in 1900 for John H. Robinson, a city/county clerk who was murdered mysteriously in 1926. Over 1,000 persons came to pay their respects at his wake, which was held in the parlor of his home. Rumor has it that his friendly ghost, named "the Boogie Man," occasionally returns to the tiny turreted room upstairs.

In 1994, the home was converted to a charming bed-and-breakfast. Four guest rooms are in the main house. The original carriage house, tack house, and studio have been transformed into cheerful cottages separate from the main house; they feature kitchens and amenities designed for longer stays. Inside the 3,800-square-foot main house, the high-ceilinged guest rooms feature pocket doors, wood floors, fireplaces, bay windows, and handsome period pieces. Arcana, one of the romantic upstairs guest rooms, has a bay window with a view of Thumb Butte. The equally delightful Arcadia has its original claw-foot bathtub.

Breakfast is served downstairs in the sun-filled dining room, where you can greet the day with steaming cups of freshly ground Mount Vernon Coffee, the inn's own special blend.

Rates

The four guest rooms are available for $90 and the three cottages for $100 to $120; special weekly and monthly rates are offered. Breakfast and afternoon refreshments are included in the guest-room rates only. Visa, MasterCard, and Discover are accepted. Check-in is from 3 P.M. to 8 P.M. and check-out at 11 A.M. No pets are allowed. Smoking is permitted in designated outdoor areas only.

Amenities

All rooms have private baths and telephones. The rooms share a parlor, a sitting room, and a VCR. The guest rooms have queen-size beds, ceiling fans, and data access. The cottages have standard double and queen-size beds, fully equipped kitchens, televisions, and air conditioners.

Location

The inn is at the corner of Mount Vernon Avenue and Willis Street in Prescott. After dark, look for the glowing stained-glass windows at the top of the turret.

Pleasant Street Inn Bed-and-Breakfast

Pleasant Street Inn Bed-and-Breakfast

142 South Pleasant Street
Prescott, Arizona 86303
phone: 520-445-4774
Jean Urban, owner/innkeeper

HISTORIC HOMES HAVE ALWAYS BEEN TREASURED in Prescott, even to the point of moving them up a hill for preservation's sake. That's just what happened to the stately structure that houses the Pleasant Street Inn Bed-and-Breakfast. This handsome New England–style home was built in 1906 on the downtown lot now occupied by the Prescott Police Department. In 1990, it was carefully transported a few blocks up the street to the town's Victorian neighborhood to replace a 19th-century home destroyed by fire.

In its original downtown setting, the two-story frame structure housed a beauty shop in what is today the inn's sitting room. Later, it served as the city's group home for mentally disabled adults. In 1991, it was sold to Jean Urban, an escapee from the corporate world in Phoenix who relocated to Prescott for its sense of history. The enterprising Urban immediately began transforming her transplanted historic structure into an inviting bed-and-breakfast.

The Pleasant Street Inn, painted a soft gray and trimmed in sparkling white, is named for the street on which it stands. But it's also true that the word *pleasant* perfectly describes the inn's home-away-from-home atmosphere. Unlike many fussy Victorian structures, the rooms at this inn are bright and airy, a result of the many added and enlarged windows. An uncluttered, almost contemporary feeling exists throughout the main living areas, where plush gray wall-to-wall carpeting and crisp white walls add a feeling of newness. Traditional style is not forgotten, however. You'll see it in the gracious living room, where high-backed upholstered wing chairs are paired in front of the bay window. Within view is the fireplace, where smoldering cedar logs scent the air. In the morning, breakfast is served in the dining room atop the gleaming oak table and pine sideboard, unless guests prefer the outdoor setting of the adjacent covered porch.

Three of the inn's four guest rooms are located upstairs. The largest is a romantic corner two-room suite featuring a sitting room, a fireplace, and a bay window. All the guest rooms have private baths and are furnished with colorful floral-print quilts and lace curtains. The elegant Terrace Suite, located downstairs on the main level, is named for the private covered deck that adjoins the two-room suite; the cozy sitting room features a sofa bed and doubles as a second bedroom, which makes this a favorite choice for families with children.

The inn is conveniently located a few blocks from the center of historic downtown Prescott within walking distance of Courthouse Plaza and the antique shops, cafes, and boutiques of this favorite weekend escape.

Rates

The two rooms and the pair of two-room suites are available for $85 to $125 (double occupancy). Full breakfast, afternoon refreshments, and hors d'oeuvres are included. MasterCard, Visa, and Discover are accepted. No smoking is permitted indoors. Pets are not allowed. Off-street parking is available.

Prescott Pines Inn

901 White Spar Road (AZ 89 South)
Prescott, Arizona 86303
phone: 800-541-5374 or 520-445-7270
fax: 520-778-3665
Jean Wu and Michael Acton, owners/innkeepers

AS FITS ITS NAME, the Prescott Pines Inn sits in the trees on a pine-studded acre of land. It is located at the edge of Prescott National Forest a little over a mile from downtown. This site was the location of a dairy farm where a Mormon farmer named Haymore built his residence in 1902. His family included 15 children, which may explain why three smaller structures were added alongside the family home. The original four buildings remain on the property today.

In 1933, the Haymore homestead was converted into a motel, complete with a neon sign out front. The guest quarters were decidedly dark, with wood-paneled walls and brown carpets. Photos taken during those "motel days" hang in the inn's dining room today. In the early 1980s, a couple named Young purchased the old motel and began a massive remodeling project to transform the historic buildings into a country-style bed-and-breakfast. When the inn opened in 1985, a charming Victorian-style porch stretched across the front of the main building and a newly expanded kitchen was at the back. The rooms had been repainted, redecorated, and refurbished, and the exterior sparkled in its new coat of paint. A white picket fence framed the front yard, and a handsome wooden sign had replaced the old neon one.

In 1987, the inn was sold to current owners Jean Wu and Michael Acton, who have added their own Victorian touches. Their creative efforts have enhanced the appeal of this charming country retreat, which is painted Cape Cod gray and trimmed in white. The inn's 13 guest rooms are located in four separate guesthouses. Due to the land's sloping contour, the guesthouses sit at different levels: one is nestled under ponderosa pines, another is tucked beneath cedars, and one borders a flagstone patio and garden.

Each guest room is named after a flower, like Morning Glory, Larkspur, and Columbine. The names appear on hand-painted ceramic door plates. Each room has a ground-level porch and a private bath and is tastefully decorated with oak and pine furnishings, period wallpaper, and lace curtains. The rooms are also equipped with phones, color cable television, and alarm clocks. The largest units have kitchenettes.

Prescott Pines Inn

The office is located in the historic two-story main house. Double entry doors and large windows overlook a landscaped front yard with a fountain and rose gardens. Located adjacent to the lobby, the dining room features gleaming plank floors and a wood-burning fireplace which provides a warm welcome to guests on winter mornings. The innkeepers' delicious full breakfasts are served on twin oak tables set with rose-patterned china. Breakfast is optional and must be reserved in advance for either of the two seatings, one designed for early birds and the other for those who like to linger.

Rates

The 13 rooms are available for $59 to $199. Optional breakfast is $5 per person; advance reservations are required. MasterCard and Visa are accepted. No pets are allowed. Smoking is not permitted.

Amenities

The guest rooms have queen- or king-size beds, private baths, direct-dial phones, color cable television, and digital alarm clocks; some have kitchenettes and fireplaces. A two-bedroom chalet accommodates eight persons. A gift shop is on the premises. Convenient parking is provided. The inn offers complimentary pickup at the local airport and the bus station.

Location

From Courthouse Plaza in downtown Prescott, follow Montezuma Street south for 1.3 miles; it becomes White Spar Road (AZ 89 South). The inn is on the left.

Victorian Inn of Prescott

Victorian Inn of Prescott

246 South Cortez Street
Prescott, Arizona 86303
phone: 520-778-2642
Tamia Thunstedt, owner/innkeeper

THIS VICTORIAN MANSION, painted bright blue and trimmed with white, sits on a quiet corner a block from Courthouse Plaza in downtown Prescott. It was built in 1893 by attorney John C. Herndon, who designed his elegant residence in the Queen Anne style with bay windows, gingerbread trim, and second-story peak-roofed turret. Herndon's undertaking was an elaborate one from the start. He hauled in lumber and hand-tooled woodwork by train from the East and outfitted the interior with oak banisters, stained-glass windows, and ornate chandeliers. These distinctive touches are still in place today, thanks to a careful restoration project which took place during the 1980s, before the home was opened as a bed-and-breakfast.

If you feel like you've been whisked back to the previous century when you step inside the inn, that's just the way owner/innkeeper Tamia Thunstedt planned it. The Victorian period is highly regarded in Prescott, a place known as "the West's Most Eastern Town." Most of the inn's antique furnishings date to the 1800s. The floral wall coverings are exact reproductions.

The largest of the inn's four upstairs guest rooms is the bay-windowed Victoriana Suite. This original master suite is where, in 1914, John Herndon's first child was reportedly born. The spacious room features a private bath, a fireplace, a comfortable sitting area, and romantic 1860 walnut furnishings.

Down the hall are three guest rooms, each reflecting the favorite style of the late 1800s. In the cozy Teddy Bear Room, stuffed bears are piled atop an antique mahogany four-poster bed. The Rose Room boasts a brass bed and antique lace curtains. In sunny Eve's Garden Room, with its wicker furniture and canopy bed draped with chiffon, the mood is romantic. These three guest rooms share a carpeted bath with a claw-foot tub and a hand-held brass showerhead.

Breakfast, an elegant affair served on antique china with fine linens, would make Queen Victoria swoon. It's a gourmet delight, pleasing to the eye as well as the palate. Among its features are fresh fruit, home-made breads, and entrées prepared from recipes handed down through generations of the owner's Swedish family. If the weather is warm, the front porch is a perfect place to enjoy a last cup of coffee or tea and watch the town come to life.

Rates

The four guest rooms are available for $90 to $145. Full breakfast is included. MasterCard and Visa are accepted. Check-in is between 3 P.M. and 6 P.M. and check-out at 11 A.M. No pets are allowed. Smoking is not permitted indoors.

White Mountains Lakeside / Pinetop

The Coldstream Bed-and-Breakfast

P.O. Box 2988
3042 Mark Twain Drive
Pinetop, Arizona 85935
phone: 520-369-0115
Cindy and Jeff Northrup, innkeepers

SIMPLY DRIVING INTO the pine-scented town of Pinetop in the heart of the White Mountains should give you reason enough to unwind and relax. But if you need more, the sign at the entrance to The Coldstream Bed-and-Breakfast instructs you to drop your cares in the "Worry Box" at the front door so they'll not bother you during your stay.

The unhistoric-looking structure that houses The Coldstream actually dates to the 1920s. The two-story home was built as a private residence for a lumbermill owner in Cooley (now McNary), located seven miles

The Coldstream Bed-and-Breakfast

away. The clapboard home was later purchased by the Apache Lumber Company and served as a guesthouse for distinguished visitors. No doubt, if the old walls could talk, they'd probably tell of deals between governors and other state officials who came to view the forestry operations that were so vital to Arizona's economy.

The house was moved to its present three-and-a-half-acre site in a residential neighborhood near Pinetop Country Club when the land lease from the White Mountains Apache tribe expired in 1980. It was converted into a bed-and-breakfast in 1992 and sold to the current owners in 1994. Remodeling efforts through the years have resulted in an additional porch, a brick fireplace, a flagstone patio, and an enclosed hot tub. Today, the inviting country inn continues to draw those seeking to escape their cares and worries in the refreshing mountain air of ponderosa-pine country.

The inn's five guest rooms, located on both floors, feature elegant furnishings and are named after lumber camps that dotted the area a century ago. The largest, the Cooley and McNary Suites, are located upstairs and share a private sitting room equipped with a television, a VCR, and a small library. Downstairs, three beautifully appointed guest rooms feature king- and queen-size beds and private baths, original polished hardwood floors, handsome pine paneling, interesting antiques, and old photographs. The spacious common room has carpeted floors, a brick fireplace, and a billiard table; it is a perfect place for thawing out after a winter day on the slopes.

A hearty country breakfast of homemade breads, hot entrées, fruits, and juices is served in the refined dining room or the sun-splashed kitchen nook overlooking the flagstone patio. The inn provides bicycles, lawn games in the summer, and stables for boarding your horse.

The White Mountains area is a playground no matter what time of year. Sunrise Park Resort, 40 minutes away, offers downhill and cross-country skiing. A number of fine golf courses and well over 50 lakes for fishing and boating are nearby. The Hon-Dah Casino is a mere three miles away.

Rates

The five rooms are available for $95 to $135. Full breakfast is included. MasterCard and Visa are accepted. Children under 11 and pets are not allowed.

Amenities

All the rooms have private baths. A television and a VCR are in the sitting room. The inn provides terry robes, social tea at 4 P.M., bicycles, horse boarding, a pool, and an outdoor spa.

Location

Turn off AZ 260 onto Buck Springs Road in the Pinetop Country Club area. Follow Buck Springs Road for 1.5 miles to Mark Twain Drive and turn right. The inn is the first house on the right.

Lakeview Lodge

Lakeview Lodge
Route 3, Box 2251
AZ 260
Lakeside, Arizona 85929
phone: 520-368-5253
Lee Ann Kirk, manager

THE MORMON PIONEERS who founded the White Mountains town of Lakeside in 1880 originally called it Fairview. The town's name was changed to Lakeside when the first in a series of reservoirs was finished. The second name proved an accurate one, as today the town seems to have as much water as land.

The Lakeview Lodge, which claims to be the oldest log lodge in Arizona, is also true to its name. Tucked among the pines on AZ 260, the area's main thoroughfare, the lodge sits across the street from a small, picturesque lake. A rustic structure with a wide, welcoming porch, the Lakeview epitomizes guests' visions of a mountain lodge.

The rugged two-story lodge was built in 1916. Today, it looks much as it did in the beginning. The stone fireplace with flagstone hearth remains the focal point of the spacious main living room. Comfortable old-fashioned sofas and high-backed leather chairs form a conversational area around the crackling fire. The ceiling soars two stories, leaving plenty of room for admiring the stuffed mountain lion mounted above the fireplace, the old-time chandelier suspended from the ceiling, and the colorful Indian blankets tacked to the log walls.

Five guest rooms are in the main lodge, one downstairs and four upstairs. All have original log walls and wood floors, private baths, and comfortable country-style and antique furnishings. The largest guest room, suitable for a family, is located upstairs to the left of the staircase; it features a cathedral ceiling, antique pieces, and quilts. The other rooms vary in size and decor and can accommodate from two to eight people. One has a four-poster brass bed and a view of the lake across the street, while another has a cozy sitting area and overlooks a campground. The lodge also offers studio-apartment-style accommodations, complete with fireplaces and kitchenettes, in cabins located behind the main building.

Thanks to the lake right on the grounds, the lodge is a favorite with fishermen and their families. The fishing is said to be good, and the day's catch is sure to taste best when cooked on the lodge's outdoor barbecue. Non-anglers can meander down the covered walkway leading from the main lodge to Coyote's Grill and Cantina to enjoy a chef-prepared meal in a log structure which dates to 1929.

Rates

Rooms in the historic lodge range from $75 to $85 and studio-apartment cabins from $59 to $69. Children are welcome. Pets are allowed in the cabins only. Major credit cards are accepted. Breakfast is not included in the above prices, but bed-and-breakfast rates can be arranged when making a reservation.

Amenities

The guest rooms have private baths and central heating. The comfortable gathering room in the lodge has a fireplace, a television, a stereo, and a VCR. Fireplaces and kitchenettes are in the cabins. A restaurant and a lake are located on the grounds.

Location

The lodge is on AZ 260 in Lakeside, 7.5 miles southeast of Show Low.

Molly Butler Lodge

Molly Butler Lodge
P.O. Box 134
Greer, Arizona 85927
phone: 520-735-7226
Sue and Jake Jacobs, owners/innkeepers

THE MOLLY BUTLER LODGE, a wooden, shingle-roofed structure in the picturesque White Mountains village of Greer, is the oldest guest lodge in Arizona. It is the former homestead of the Butler family, who arrived in the area in the 1890s. A son, John T. Butler, grew up on the homestead enjoying the surrounding lakes and pine forests and the fork of the Little Colorado River that runs in front of the lodge. His knowledge of the area made him a sought-after guide for the hunters and fishermen who began arriving in the early 1900s. John and his wife, Molly, also from a local pioneer family, were among the first to realize the region's potential as a tourist attraction. They were hardly surprised when the Greer area, with its elevation of 8,500 feet, developed into a year-round mecca for Phoenicians seeking relief from the scorching summer heat and for skiers and other snow enthusiasts in winter.

In the early days of the 20th century, the Butlers offered overnight accommodations and 25-cent meals in exchange for their guests' help with gardening, canning, and cattle-branding chores. Fearing the family would go broke running a "free" lodge, Molly officially opened the lodge as a business in 1910. The Butlers continued operating the lodge until 1974, when they sold it to Jake Jacobs and a partner, who later sold his half to Jake. Jake and his wife, Sue, have preserved Molly's name and the Butler family's tradition of warm hospitality and down-home cooking.

Accommodations at the lodge were never fancy or expensive, and they remain so today. They were good enough for writer Zane Grey, who undoubtedly found inspiration for his novels in the lodge's natural setting and its views of lush meadows, forests, and mountains. The prolific author ate at Molly's and bunked in the old wooden "long house," the same structure that today houses eight of the lodge's 12 guest rooms. The building has been spruced up a bit with a green exterior, crisp white walls with stenciled borders in the guest rooms, and private bathrooms. Instead of bunks, there are sturdy double beds covered with hand-pieced quilts. Each room has separate heating controls. The other four guest rooms are in an adjacent building which replaced the burned original; it is attached to the lodge's lounge and dining rooms.

In keeping with the rustic atmosphere of the guest quarters, meals at the lodge are hearty, old-fashioned, and no-nonsense, just the way they were served when Molly Butler ran the kitchen.

Rates

The 12 rooms are available for $30 to $45. A two-night minimum stay is required on weekends and a three-night stay on holidays. Major credit cards are accepted. Children are welcome. There is a $10 charge for well-behaved pets.

Amenities

The rooms have private baths. The lodge offers a restaurant, a lounge, and off-street parking.

Location
The lodge is approximately 15 miles west of Springerville.
From AZ 260, turn south on AZ 373 and drive
three miles to Greer. The lodge is on the main road
through town, on the right.

White Mountain Lodge

P.O. Box 143
140 Main Street
Greer, Arizona 85927
phone: 520-735-7568
fax: 520-735-7498
Mary and Charlie Bast, owners/innkeepers

BUILT IN 1892, the White Mountain Lodge is considered the oldest structure still standing in the picturesque Greer Valley. At first, the two-story log house, constructed of timbers from the surrounding area, served mainly as the summer residence of the William Lund family, one of the first Mormon families to settle in Greer. In 1904, the house was passed on to Lund's son, Marion, upon his marriage. Marion and his wife, Agnes, converted the former vacation home into a year-round residence. They farmed the land, raised eight children, and expanded their home as needed through the years. When Marion retired from farming in 1940, the property was sold and transformed into the White Mountain Lodge by the new owners.

For more than a half-century, the White Mountain Lodge has been a year-round getaway for hiking and fishing enthusiasts in spring and cross-country and downhill skiers in winter. The Little Colorado River runs along the foot of the property. Occasionally, deer, elk, and antelope come to graze in the meadows.

Current owners Mary and Charlie Bast purchased the lodge in 1993 and filled the rooms with an interesting assortment of antiques. Guests

White Mountain Lodge

enter the lodge through a small office and reception area built at the front of the structure in 1981 to replace the original porch. Beyond the office is the lodge's main gathering area, a pine-paneled living room where comfortable armchairs and sofas are grouped in front of a stone fireplace and Southwestern paintings decorate the walls. The overall effect of this charming room is one of warmth. That feeling is especially welcome during the cold months in this little mountain hamlet, which sits at an altitude of 8,525 feet.

Seven cozy guest rooms are located on the two levels of the main lodge. Most are pine-paneled and carpeted and feature quilts and country accents. Each has an individual heating unit and a private bath with a claw-foot tub. The lodge also offers three separate one- or two-bedroom cabins with fireplaces or wood stoves. These are ideal for guests who prefer to do their own cooking and housekeeping, though cabin occupants may also arrange for bed-and-breakfast rates. Each afternoon, guests are invited to help themselves to complimentary hot drinks and homemade goodies served in the main lodge.

A full home-cooked breakfast featuring such tempting entrées as

Orange Liqueur French Toast, Sundance Eggs on tortillas, and Blintz Soufflé is served in the family dining room on a red-checked tablecloth. At one end of the table, a large picture window overlooks an expanse of rolling green meadows.

The lodge's newest offering is an occasional "Mystery Weekend," during which guests assume the roles of characters involved in a mysterious murder, conveniently solved before the weekend is over.

Rates

The seven rooms in the main lodge are available to one or two persons for $50 to $70; breakfast is included. The three cabins are available to one or two persons for $75 to $95. There is a $10 charge for each additional occupant over 18 months of age. Children and small supervised pets are welcome. The lodge is open all year. Credit cards are not accepted. Check-in is from 2 P.M. to 8 P.M. and check-out at 10 A.M. For cabin guests, a two-day minimum is required on weekends and a three-day minimum on holidays.

Amenities

The rooms in the main lodge have private baths. The cabins have private baths, televisions, and kitchenettes. A television, a VCR, a fax, and a refrigerator are in the main lodge. Ponds and a river are on the property.

Location

From AZ 260, exit south on AZ 373 and drive into Greer; the road becomes Main Street as you enter the village. Look for the lodge on your left.

Paisley Corner Bed-and-Breakfast

Paisley Corner Bed-and-Breakfast

287 North Main Street
Eagar, Arizona 85925
or P.O. Box 458
Springerville, Arizona 85938
phone: 520-333-4665
Cheryl and Cletus Tisdell, owners/innkeepers

A WIDE, WELCOMING PORCH stretches across the front of this two-story red-brick home on a corner in the small mountain town of Eagar. The structure was built in 1910 in the Colonial Revival style for William F. LeSueur, a prosperous Round Valley businessman and rancher. LeSueur's wife, Elna, held an important position as well, since she was the only registered nurse in the area. With no doctors or hospitals around, Elna was chiefly responsible for delivering babies and nursing the sick.

Many of the home's original stained-glass windows, hardwood floors, and hand-carved woodwork features remain today. Paisley Corner opened as a bed-and-breakfast in 1991. Owners/innkeepers Cheryl and Cletus

Tisdell spent three years restoring the structure to its Victorian splendor. Then they furnished the rooms with period antiques and collectibles they had acquired through the years and created ceilings, borders, and wainscoting from the old hammered-tin ceilings that once hung in the Fox Theatre in Phoenix.

Breakfast is prepared on an authentic 1910 gas stove and served on an oak buffet and a lace-covered walnut table; the attending Tisdells often dress in 19th-century clothing. In the antique-filled parlor, guests are invited to unwind with a toast in front of the huge oak-and-marble fireplace. Across the hall in the soda shop, feelings of nostalgia should begin to set in as you wander about an assortment of treasures, including an old phone booth, a working antique Coke machine, and a restored 1946 Wurlitzer jukebox that plays oldies-but-goodies on 78-rpm records.

Guests are accommodated upstairs in elegant bedrooms featuring glass-paneled transoms, rose-colored carpeting, and elaborate bathrooms with claw-foot tubs, "rib cage" showers, and pull-chain commodes. Each bedroom has Victorian decor and is furnished with interesting period pieces: an oak canopy bed with matching vanity, an elegant velvet chaise lounge, a carved walnut bed with an eight-foot-high headboard, authentic steamer trunks, a lace-covered brass bed on a raised platform. Ceiling fans rotate lazily.

The perfect place to relax and view the activity on Eagar's main thoroughfare is the wooden swing on the front porch. At the side of the house is a brick courtyard surrounded by flowers. An inviting gazebo-enclosed hot tub waits in the backyard.

Rates

The five guest rooms with private baths are available for $75 to $85. Full breakfast and complimentary refreshments and pastries upon arrival are included. MasterCard and Visa are accepted. Smoking is not permitted indoors. The inn is open all year.

Alpine

Hannagan Meadow Lodge
P.O. Box 335
US 191
Alpine, Arizona 85920
phone: 800-547-1416 or 520-339-4370
Mark and Carrie Dauksavage, innkeepers

IT'S TOO BAD Hannagan Meadow Lodge didn't exist in 1540, when Spanish explorer Francisco Vasquez de Coronado led his party through the rugged White Mountains of eastern Arizona in search of the legendary Seven Cities of Cibola. He would have considered the rustic lodge in the forest a treasure indeed.

The lodge was built of native rock and logs in 1929 in a clearing overlooking a meadow. It offered weary travelers a place to rest as they made the two-day trek along the winding, narrow dirt roads the explorer once used. This historic route, now paved and named the Coronado Trail, stretches 89 miles from Alpine to Morenci and ranks as one of Arizona's most remote and scenic highways.

Hannagan Meadow Lodge

Adjacent to the lodge is the 187,000-acre Blue Range Primitive Area, one of the state's untouched wilderness areas. The lodge can thus boast one of the Southwest's most remote locations offering modern conveniences. At an elevation of 9,100 feet, it attracts summer guests seeking cool, refreshing, pine-scented breezes. In the winter when the slopes are covered with snow, skiers arrive for the high, remote back-country trails and, afterwards, the warmth of a roaring fire in the old lodge's rugged stone fireplace.

The lodge's newest reincarnation began in 1996, when the current owners tired of their early retirement, which had begun four years earlier when they won the lottery. Needing a challenge, they purchased the neglected 70-year-old complex and set about restoring the past—but not at the expense of modern convenience. They refinished the floors, improved the water and electrical systems, and refurbished the interior.

The rustic log-and-beam lodge offers guest rooms on the second floor, above the main lobby and dining room. The eight tastefully decorated rooms, furnished in an elegant country-manor style, have private baths. Some have views of the meadow across the street. The Honeymoon Suite, the largest room in the lodge, features a king-size rice bed and a small private veranda. Off the road a short walk from the lodge are two single and three duplex log cabins. All have fireplaces, plank floors, log- or wood-paneled walls, and private baths.

Although the guests rooms and cabins offer many amenities and are attractive and comfortably furnished, don't expect to find a television or a VCR. There's too much to do outdoors. Surrounded by solitude, many guests are happy to simply sit on the spacious front porch and watch hummingbirds dart from feeder to feeder. Some come to pick wild berries and mushrooms or to photograph the wildflowers and wildlife that abound in the area. For those preferring more strenuous activity, there is horseback riding, mountain biking, hunting, fishing, and skiing in winter. This is a perfect getaway for those seeking to reunite with nature.

Rates

Rooms in the lodge are available for $50 to $125; breakfast is included. The cabins rent for $60 to $95. Children are welcome.

Amenities

The guest rooms have private baths, and the cabins have private baths and fireplaces. The restaurant is open to the public for breakfast, lunch, and dinner. A general store and horse stables are on the premises. Hiking trails are nearby.

Location

The lodge is 22 miles south of Alpine on US 191.

Kay El Bar Guest Ranch

Kay El Bar Guest Ranch

P.O. Box 2480
Wickenburg, Arizona 85358
phone: 520-684-7593
Jane Nash and Jan Martin, owners

PERHAPS IF WICKENBURG cattle rancher and entertainer Romaine Lowdermilk had had his way back in 1903, the Kay El Bar Guest Ranch would have a different name today. Lowdermilk wanted his cattle brand to read *LK*, for the first and last letters of his last name. But that brand was already registered, and he had to find another. He reversed the letters to *KL*, added a bar, and created the brand and name still used at the ranch today.

At the beginning, the Lowdermilk family's one-room adobe residence was the only livable structure on the ranch. An adobe two-bedroom cottage was built in 1914, and the remaining buildings were added in 1925. A year later, the compound opened as a dude ranch. It had a living room and an office in the main lodge and eight guest rooms and a two-bedroom cottage across the way. Accommodations at the ranch are much the same today except for the swimming pool, which was added behind the main lodge in 1958.

A new chapter for the Kay El Bar began in 1980, when two sisters from Phoenix, Jane Nash and Jan Martin, and their husbands purchased the property. Jane and Jan chose this ranch beside the Hassayampa River at the base of the Bradshaw Mountains to accommodate their husbands' jobs in Phoenix, a 60-mile drive. Motivated by childhood memories of good times spent on dude ranches, Jane and Jan had often dreamed of owning and operating their own ranch. The Kay El Bar, a National Historic Site and one of Arizona's oldest and smallest guest ranches, is their dream come true.

The Kay El Bar's tradition as a friendly, family-style dude ranch with a focus on ridin' and relaxin' continues today. With its 60 acres of scenic desert foothills bordered by federal land, there are plenty of trails for horseback riding and hiking. Relaxing is as easy as lounging in the shade of a towering eucalyptus tree or sinking into a comfortable couch in the spacious, rustic living room. A fire is usually crackling in the old stone fireplace. Overhead, you can see the rough ceiling beams that once served as telegraph poles between Phoenix and Wickenburg. The lodge's eight guest rooms are down the hall from the living room. Each features Western decor, a private bath, the original 14-inch-thick adobe walls, and refinished 1920 Monterey furnishings.

One of the best things about a ranch vacation is knowing that jeans are appropriate for just about every activity. You can even wear your favorite denims at mealtime, which is announced with the clang of an old railroad bell. The ranch's excellent cuisine, served family-style in the dining room, is worth writing home about. And the photos of old cowboy stars and other famous faces which line the walls are worth a closer look.

Rates

The one-person rate for the eight rooms in the lodge is $120 per day to $810 per week. The two-person rate for the two-bedroom, two-bath cottage with living room and fireplace is $240 per day to $1,640 per week. All meals, horseback riding, outdoor games, and use of the pool and other facilities are included. The ranch is open from mid-October to May 1. A two-night minimum stay is required from mid-October to February 15 and a four-night minimum stay from February 15 to May 1. Personal checks, Visa, and MasterCard are accepted. Children are welcome, but pets are not.

Amenities

The ranch offers horseback riding, hiking trails, a heated swimming pool, a dining room, private baths, and a television and phone in the main lodge.

Location

The ranch is approximately four miles north of downtown Wickenburg. Follow AZ 89 / US 93 for two miles to Lincoln Road. Turn right and drive two miles to the ranch; the last mile is on a dirt road.

Sombrero Ranch Bed-and-Breakfast

Sombrero Ranch Bed-and-Breakfast
31910 West Bralliar Road
Wickenburg, Arizona 85390
phone: 520-684-0222
fax: 520-684-7100
Peter Nufer, innkeeper

FROM THE PICTURE WINDOW in the Sombrero Ranch's spacious dining room, you can see Vulture Peak in the distance. This landmark is where
prospector Henry Wickenburg discovered gold in 1863 and established
the Vulture Mine, which later became the richest gold mine in Arizona.
This inn's lofty perch atop a hill on 49 acres of desert landscape allows a
360-degree view which sweeps across downtown Wickenburg, a rolling
country club, and the surrounding mountains.

The adobe ranch-style home was built in 1937 by Harvey Smith, whose
photographs, taken during various stages of the house's construction, line
the corridor in the guest wing. Another interesting relic is the architect's
rendering of the house, on display in the dining room. The ranch remained a private residence through four owners before being sold in 1994
to Peter Nufer, a native of Switzerland, who ended a year-long tour across

the United States at this hilltop house in Wickenburg. After spending nearly two years refurbishing rooms, landscaping, and building his owner's quarters, he opened the 5,000-square-foot structure as a bed-and-breakfast with four guests rooms and a separate guesthouse at the rear for lengthier stays.

Throughout the airy home, the owner has cleverly managed to maintain the ambiance of the old Southwest while integrating touches of the new. The exterior resembles a Spanish hacienda, with its white adobe walls and red-tile roof. Inside, original arched entryways, thick adobe walls, and beam ceilings bring back the 1930s and blend well with today's Berber carpets and new lodgepole-pine beds. The gracious living room has a tiled fireplace and a wagon-wheel chandelier, and the adjacent corner sunroom is furnished in bright white wicker. The guest wing is located off the living room. The immaculate, well-appointed rooms have private baths and queen-size beds. A door from the guest-wing corridor opens to a quiet courtyard and a path leading to a kidney-shaped swimming pool and a private screened-in ramada. And everywhere on the property, the view lends a top-of-the-world feeling.

The morning starts with breakfast served in the dining room on the ranch's original 14-foot oak table, where the host wows his guests with a variety of irresistible dishes, like puffy Belgian waffles topped with luscious strawberries and fresh whipped cream or a delicious Southwestern quiche. Afterwards, hardy types can walk the mile into town to poke about the antique stores and tour Wickenburg's Desert Caballeros Western Museum.

Rates

The four rooms rent for $75. A deluxe continental breakfast is included. MasterCard and Visa are accepted. The ranch is closed July and August.

Litchfield Park

The Wigwam Resort
300 Indian School Road
Litchfield Park, Arizona 85340
phone: 800-327-0396 or 602-935-3811
fax: 602-935-3737

THE STORY of the luxurious Wigwam Resort began with an old rubber tire. Of course, the heavy-duty tire designed in 1915 by Paul Litchfield, a vice president of the Goodyear Tire and Rubber Company, was no ordinary tire. It required a particular type of high-grade cotton that was hard to import during World War I. Because Arizona's climate seemed ideal for growing the long-staple cotton, Goodyear began sowing cotton seeds along the Agua Fria River in 1916. The cotton-growing venture led to the eventual transformation of a desolate desert into a 38,000-acre landscaped empire named Litchfield Park.

The Wigwam Resort

In 1919, what Goodyear called the "Organization House" was constructed to accommodate executives and specialists from the company's Ohio headquarters. The two-story Pueblo-style adobe structure, affectionately dubbed "The Wigwam," remained a company operation until 1929, when it was opened to the public as The Wigwam Resort, with accommodations for 24 guests. During the 1930s and 1940s, several clusters of new buildings called "Wickiups" were raised in front of the original structure, and a golf course was added. During World War II, the resort grew to accommodate 110 guests and provided housing for military personnel at nearby Luke Air Force Base.

Expansions and improvements continued through the years, earning the lush 450-acre desert retreat numerous awards, including the prestigious Mobil Five Star rating for 22 years. In 1986, a $45 million refurbishment project was launched by the new owner, the SunCor Development Company. When the resort was sold again in 1990, a 10,800-square-foot ballroom and 90 courtyard villas were added. Today, The Wigwam Resort boasts 331 rooms, three 18-hole golf courses, a clubhouse, a tennis center, two swimming pools, three restaurants, a ballroom, a conference center, and 26,000 square feet of outdoor patios and party lawns.

The original hacienda style has been preserved throughout the elegant low-rise resort, where the decor reflects the cowboy-and-Indian influence of Arizona's territorial days. Interesting photographs dating to the resort's beginnings line the halls and walls in the historic section of the main lodge. The rustic Fireplace Room, with its thick adobe walls and rugged ceiling beams, is a favorite among guests, who like to thumb through the excellent collection of classics in the adjoining library before curling up to read in front of the brick fireplace. The spacious guest "casitas" are arranged in a village setting amid lush lawns, towering palms, and blooming flower beds. The oversized accommodations—reminiscent of the resort's early years, when extended stays were common—feature custom Southwestern furnishings, private patios, and all the amenities you might expect at an elegant, award-winning resort.

Rates

The 331 rooms are available for $126 to $446, depending on the season; high season runs from January 1 to April 30. Major credit cards are accepted. Pets are allowed with a $50 deposit.

Amenities

The rooms have telephones, data ports, cable television, and free movies. The resort offers three golf courses, two pools, conference facilities, nine tennis courts, a health club, a gift shop, a salon, three restaurants, a lounge, a ballroom, and concierge service.

Location

The resort is in Litchfield Park, 25 minutes west of Phoenix's Sky Harbor International Airport. Exit Interstate 10 at Litchfield Road. Turn right (north) and drive 2.4 miles to Indian School Road (not the Indian School Road bypass). Turn right (east) and go a block and a half to The Wigwam's main entrance.

Marriott's Camelback Inn

5402 East Lincoln Drive
Scottsdale, Arizona 85253
phone: 800-24CAMEL or 602-948-1700
fax: 602-951-2152

DURING THE 1920S AND 1930S, elegant resorts began to appear around the Phoenix Valley, offering well-heeled Easterners a pleasant escape from the cold winter climate. One of the first was the Camelback Inn, which joined the Scottsdale resort scene in 1936. It featured 75 petite, smartly furnished adobe cottages (each named for a different species of cactus), fine dining, and top-notch entertainment. After more than half a century of continuous operation, the Camelback Inn is Scottsdale's only authentic Southwestern resort.

The inn was the brainchild of Jack Stewart, former manager of another Phoenix resort. He enlisted the financial aid of John C. Lincoln, then president of the Cleveland Electric Company in Ohio. Later, Stewart and his wife, Louise, purchased the resort. They agreed with the nondrinking Lincolns that the resort should never have a bar. Guests felt differently, however, and within two years of the inn's opening, a bar was built separate from the main lobby.

A success from the start, the inn was expanded to 118 rooms under Stewart's guidance. It became a popular spot with celebrities and dignitaries, including Dwight and Mamie Eisenhower, Jimmy Stewart, Bette Davis, and J. C. Penney. Another frequent guest was J. W. Marriott, Sr., who bought the inn from the Stewarts in 1967, launching the Marriott Corporation's resort network. Under Marriott ownership, the inn has expanded to 424 guest "casitas" and continues to attract the stars. Johnny Carson, Reba McEntire, Oprah Winfrey, and Don Shula have all been guests.

Marriott's Camelback Inn

High above the inn's main entrance are the words "Where time stands still," a worthy motto for a place interested in pampering guests and showcasing its Arizona history. At the award-winning 125-acre desert retreat nestled between Camelback and Mummy Mountain, efforts have been made to preserve the ambiance of the desert Southwest. A step into the 60-year-old lobby—with its original flagstone floors, adobe walls, carved-wood chandelier and ceiling beams, and beehive fireplace—is indeed a step back in time. The adobe guest casitas and suites feature Native American artwork, Indian-print furnishings, and copper panels. They also have private entrances, garden patios, and balconies.

After a recent multimillion-dollar refurbishing project, the celebrated inn today offers swimming pools, golf courses, tennis courts, a jogging and cycling path, a playground, a 27,000-square-foot spa, and award-winning restaurants. A small adobe chapel near the main entrance was built in 1959 as a memorial to John C. Lincoln, making the Camelback Inn the only Arizona resort to have its own chapel.

History is still in the making at this resort, which has received the prestigious Mobil Five Star rating for 27 consecutive years and the AAA Five Diamond Award for two decades.

Paradise Valley

Hermosa Inn

**5532 North Palo Cristi Road
Paradise Valley, Arizona 85253
phone: 800-241-1210 or 602-955-8614
fax: 602-955-8299
Fred and Jennifer Unger, owners**

IN 1930, WHEN COWBOY ARTIST Alonzo "Lon" Megargee spotted the
wide-open desert bordered by mountains far from the city of Phoenix,

he knew he was home. The raw-boned broncobuster, stud-poker dealer, and commercial artist—best remembered for his paintings *Black Bart* and *A Cowboy's Dream* and for designing the cowboy logo for Stetson Hats—had traveled to the West from Philadelphia at the turn of the century. He ended his search for the American dream and began constructing a one-room studio. Megargee added rooms to the original structure, using adobe blocks mixed on the site and old beams from Mexico. Influenced by architecture he had studied in Spain and Mexico, he worked without formal plans as he created the unique Southwestern home he called Casa Hermosa, which means "beautiful house."

As the casa grew and his need for income increased, Megargee began operating his property as a guest ranch. Rumors of late-night gambling sessions brought surprise visits from the sheriff, so Megargee thoughtfully provided guests with secret tunnels from the main house to the stables, where they could discretely disappear. By 1941, he was forced to put his beloved casa, filled with his art and furnishings, up for sale.

Through the years, the sprawling structure adapted to new roles under a succession of owners. A pool, tennis courts, and more casitas and villas were added, and private residences began to appear in the wide-open spaces Megargee had prized. A devastating fire in 1987 damaged his old home. It was saved when current owners Fred and Jennifer Unger bought the property in 1992 and decided to restore its original charm.

Hermosa Inn

Photographs and prints of Megargee's artwork hang inside his old home, now called the Hermosa Inn. The reception area and a popular restaurant and bar now occupy the original structure, where the aged adobe walls and original ironwork reflect the Southwestern ambiance of the 1930s. Considered one of the few remaining authentic Southwestern haciendas, the single-story inn features 35 individually decorated casitas scattered over six and a half acres of desert gardens, green lawns, and flower beds.

The accommodations range from a spacious 1,700-square-foot villa with a beehive fireplace, a skylight, and a large patio to a cozy hand-built adobe room with a sitting area. The luxurious appointments include large Southwestern-style wooden armoires and hand-painted Mexican tiles. Most rooms have a fireplace and a private patio.

This secluded desert hideaway attracts corporate retreats and those looking for an intimate escape—including Megargee himself, who died in 1960 but is reported to return for occasional visits to his beloved Casa Hermosa.

Rates

Rooms are available for $89 to $500 per night, depending on the season. High season is from November 22 through April 21. Continental breakfast is included. Credit cards are accepted.

Amenities

The guest rooms have color televisions, telephones, and private baths. Most have private patios and beehive fireplaces, and some have wet bars or kitchenettes. A health club, a swimming pool, a Jacuzzi, tennis courts, a restaurant, and a bar are on the property.

Location

The entrance to the inn is on North Palo Cristi Road. From Lincoln Drive, turn south on North Palo Cristi and follow it to the inn, located on the right. From Camelback Road, turn north on 44th Street, then turn left at Stanford and follow it to North Palo Cristi and the inn.

Arizona Biltmore

Arizona Biltmore

24th Street and Missouri Avenue
Phoenix, Arizona 85016
phone: 800-950-0086 or 602-955-6600
fax: 602-381-7600

A PHOENIX LANDMARK for more than 65 years, the internationally renowned Arizona Biltmore is snugly burrowed into the foothills of Squaw Peak on 39 acres of exquisitely landscaped grounds. Inspired by consulting architect Frank Lloyd Wright, this grande dame of Arizona resorts was constructed in 1929 of blocks molded on the site and cast with geometric patterns. The hotel was purchased by Chicago chewing-gum magnate William Wrigley, Jr., in 1930. During the following 44 years of operation under the Wrigley family, the Biltmore gained a reputation as an international resort.

Dignitaries and celebrities from around the world have been attracted to the "Jewel of the Desert" since its beginnings. Edna Ferber penned several novels while a guest at the Biltmore, and Irving Berlin wrote "White Christmas" during his stay. Clark Gable reportedly lost his wedding ring on the golf course. Harpo Marx and his bride honeymooned at the Biltmore, as did Ronald and Nancy Reagan. Other famous people who have stayed at the Biltmore include the duke and duchess of Windsor, Henry Kissinger, Marilyn Monroe, and every president of the United States since its opening.

In 1973, shortly after the Wrigley family sold the hotel to Talley Industries, a six-alarm fire spread through the structure, which was then closed for refurbishing. During the reconstruction of the damaged floors, cement blocks were again molded on-site in an effort to preserve the building's architectural integrity.

Expansions and enhancements have continued through the years, the most recent a $50 million project by the current owner, Grossman Company Properties. Today, the Arizona Biltmore is a luxurious playground that pampers its guests with 600 rooms, two PGA golf courses, an 18-hole putting course, three restaurants, a conference center, an athletic club and spa, lighted tennis courts, five heated pools, and a pool complex with private cabanas and a 92-foot water slide.

The Biltmore's patterned cement blocks, geometric stained glass, and 200-foot lobby with gilt ceiling must have presented a challenge to interior designers. Sofas and armchairs of wicker and rattan, birdcages, and Southwestern pottery add whimsical and softening touches throughout the otherwise austere structure's interior, and the 250,000 bulbs planted annually on the manicured grounds add exciting splashes of color. The guest rooms feature Mission-style furnishings in restful tones of beige, sand, and ivory.

This luxurious escape is full of delightful surprises, including the story of the famous sprites—the cluster of concrete female figures standing guard near the entrance. Though they look perfectly suited to their site, they were actually designed by Frank Lloyd Wright in 1914 for Chicago's Midway Gardens and moved to the Biltmore in 1982.

Rates

The 600 guest rooms include 50 villas and 100 rooms for nonsmokers. They are available for $115 to $1,670, depending on the season and/or package. The resort is open year-round.

Amenities

All rooms have private baths, two telephones, a television, a mini-bar, a desk, and a security system. Most have a balcony or patio. The resort offers three restaurants, two bars, two 18-hole golf courses, an 18-hole putting course, eight tennis courts, five swimming pools, a water slide, an athletic club, room service, and a concierge. It is within walking distance of fashionable shopping and within 15 minutes of Sky Harbor International Airport.

Location

The resort is in the heart of Phoenix's prestigious Biltmore District. The entrance is at 24th Street and Missouri Avenue.

Maricopa Manor Bed-and-Breakfast Inn

15 West Pasadena Avenue
Phoenix, Arizona 85013
phone: 800-292-6403 or 602-274-6302
fax: 602-266-3904
Paul and Mary Ellen Kelley, innkeepers

THIS WHITE SPANISH MISSION Revival structure with arched openings and a Mexican red-tile roof was built in 1928 on what was then a quiet country road five miles from downtown Phoenix. The stucco-on-adobe home was constructed as a summer residence for Phoenix city dwellers Byron Showers, an agricultural engineer, and his wife, Naomi. Five years later, they moved from the city to their vacation home and made it a permanent residence.

Maricopa Manor
Bed-and-Breakfast Inn

Things are different today. A multistory office building looms nearby, and traffic whizzes a block away. But you'd hardly know it at the Maricopa Manor Bed-and-Breakfast Inn, where all is as quiet and serene as a place in the country.

This inn's tranquil atmosphere is the result of clever planning and hard work by current owners Mary Ellen and Paul Kelley, a couple from Atlanta who purchased the home in 1970. To accommodate their large family, which consisted of three of their own children and nine foster children, they enlarged rooms in the original structure and attached a two-story addition at the back. Later, they acquired the house next door, added a guesthouse, and walled the entire one-acre lot. By the time the brood was gone from the nest, the Kelleys were determined to keep their sprawling compound filled with the activity they had become accustomed to. In 1989, they opened a bed-and-breakfast.

The inn's overall feeling is that of a secluded oasis. Trellised brick pathways draped with blooming bougainvillea lead beside romantic gardens and patios to the pool area, where colorful flowers and lush greenery explode and tumble from terra-cotta pots. Hand-painted Mexican tiles decorate the pool and the trickling tiered fountains. In a cozy redwood gazebo, a hot tub beckons. And everywhere is the sweet aroma of citrus blossoms.

The main house has a variety of gracious common rooms, each furnished with antiques and interesting items from the Kelleys' collection. In the living room, velvet love seats which once graced Barry Goldwater's home are paired with Louis XVI tables made in France in the 1700s. A striking painting depicting the naming of Phoenix in 1867 hangs above a carved marble fireplace, and Moorish-style columns and archways lead to adjacent rooms. The casual gathering room with redwood-beam cathedral ceiling was once the focal point for family life. Now, it's a favorite with guests, who assemble here in the afternoons for beverages and home-baked treats.

The five self-contained guests suites are designed to provide the utmost in comfort and privacy. Two are located in the main house, and the other three are just steps away. All are spacious and feature private baths, televisions, telephones, an abundance of books, and cozy breakfast areas. Some have wood-burning or gas fireplaces, canopy beds, and private outdoor entrances.

Morning at Maricopa Manor begins with Mary Ellen's gentle tap on your door at the requested time. The knock announces the arrival of breakfast, delivered in an enormous wicker basket filled with scrumptious homemade goodies and fresh orange juice squeezed from trees in the yard.

Rates

The four one-bedroom suites and one two-bedroom suite are available for $89 to $159. Full breakfast is included. Limited smoking is allowed. Reservations are required. Major credit cards are accepted. No pets are permitted.

Amenities

The rooms have wheelchair access, private baths, color televisions, and telephones. The inn offers common areas, a courtyard, a heated pool, a hot tub, and gardens. Afternoon refreshments are served daily.

Location

The inn is in north-central Phoenix. From the intersection of Camelback Road and Central Avenue, go north on Central for one block to Pasadena Avenue. Turn left (west) and watch for Maricopa Manor on the left.

Royal Palms

Royal Palms
5200 East Camelback Road
Phoenix, Arizona 85018
phone: 800-672-6011 or 602-840-3610
fax: 602-840-6927
Fred and Jennifer Unger, owners

WHEN THE ELEGANT ROYAL PALMS opened its doors in 1948, the structure at the base of Camelback Mountain was already considered a local landmark.

The sprawling 3,500-square-foot Spanish Revival villa was built in 1926 as the winter home of Delos Willard Cooke, a New York industrialist and financier, and his wife, Florence. The stunning mansion had plastered brick walls, tile roofs, elaborate wrought-iron grillwork, and romantic arched doorways. Palms lined the driveway, and citrus groves and exotic flower and cactus gardens surrounded the home.

In 1937, six years after the death of Delos Cooke, the property was sold to W. E. Travis, president of Greyhound Bus Lines. Travis sold the property a few years later after adding a second story at one side of the mansion. Eventually, the estate was purchased by former bandleader Al Stovall, who in 1948 transformed it into a luxurious inn. Named after the towering palms lining the driveway, the Royal Palms offered elegant guest rooms in the converted mansion and 15 new guest casitas west of the building. A few years later, 45 casitas were added. It was customary for well-heeled guests like Helena Rubenstein and Groucho Marx to arrive for a season at the Royal Palms, where they could play tennis and golf, ride horseback, and swim in a heart-shaped pool.

In the 1990s, the inn's original 65-acre site was reduced to nine acres when the golf course was sold to a custom builder, who planned to develop upscale homes. Fearing the demise of the historic landmark, local preservationists Fred and Jennifer Unger purchased the Royal Palms in 1995. The Ungers were no strangers to the challenges of reviving historic buildings, having recently completed the successful restoration of the Hermosa Inn in Paradise Valley, another historic escape featured in this book.

The same towering palms that greeted visitors to the Cooke mansion in the 1920s welcome guests to the newly restored Royal Palms today. There are now 120 elegantly appointed casitas and guest rooms, a hotel nearing completion, and lush, manicured gardens, paths, courtyards, and patios surrounding the original mansion. The effect is of a serene Mediterranean villa with old stone walkways, antique fountains, and private walled gardens. Nineteen casitas—including the luxurious Presidential Suite and the glamorous Honeymoon Suite—and various garden areas were designed by members of the American Society of Interior Designers.

Many artifacts and antiques have been preserved in the original mansion, which remains the focal point at the Royal Palms. A 450-year-old fountain bubbles in the entry courtyard. Original mahogany doors open to reveal handsomely furnished rooms surrounding a central garden courtyard. A colorful mural of hand-painted tiles portraying a Spanish woman with a fan remains on the wall at the rear of the courtyard in the spot chosen by the Cookes. The mansion's original living room and guest room serve as reception areas. They have floors of wood and hand-painted tiles, which also appear around windows and doorways. Across the courtyard in the Cookes' former dining room is a spacious, newly remodeled restaurant. From the rear windows of the restaurant, Camelback Mountain glows in the sunset.

It's hardly surprising to learn that this historic escape's romantic Old World atmosphere—with trickling fountains and citrus blossoms scenting the air—is a favorite setting for weekend weddings, which are booked more than a year in advance.

Rates

The 120 casitas and guest rooms are available for $125 to $2,800, depending on the season. Major credit cards are accepted. Check-in is at 3 P.M. and check-out at noon.

Amenities

The rooms have private baths, separate showers and tubs, patios, king-size beds, color televisions, and mini-refrigerators. The inn offers a swimming pool, gardens, a restaurant with outdoor dining, a tennis court, a fitness center, salons, boardrooms, a library, a multilingual concierge staff, laundry service, and valet parking. A championship golf course is nearby. The Royal Palms is convenient to the prestigious Biltmore area and to Scottsdale, with its fashionable shopping, fine restaurants, and world-famous golf courses.

Location

The inn is in northern Phoenix on East Camelback Road between 64th and 44th Streets.

San Carlos Hotel

San Carlos Hotel
202 North Central Avenue
Phoenix, Arizona 85004
phone: 800-678-8946 or 602-253-4121
fax: 602-253-6668

WHEN THE SAN CARLOS HOTEL opened in downtown Phoenix in 1928, it was touted as one of the most modern hotels in the Southwest. With seven stories and 175 luxuriously appointed rooms, it was the capital city's first high-rise. It offered such advanced features as circulating ice water, automatic air conditioning, and elevators. Other noteworthy items were the pedestal sinks with three spigots—for hot, cold, and ice-cold water—some of which remain in the hotel today. A well dug on the property in 1874, when the city's first school occupied the site, supplied guests with ice-cold drinking water and continues to power the hotel's steam-heating and air-conditioning systems today.

Designed in the Italian Renaissance style by nationally known architects, the San Carlos was a major attraction from the start. The elegant lobby featured high, molded ceilings, terrazzo marble floors, Italian tapestries, and chandeliers of Austrian crystal. Adjoining the lobby were rooms for dancing and cards, a finely appointed bar, a dining room, and an outdoor lounge area. Elevators with gleaming copper doors transported powerbrokers, politicians, and celebrities like Clark Gable, Carole Lombard, Harry James, and Del Webb to their rooms; they are still in operation today.

A center of activity for decades, the San Carlos eventually fell into neglect and disrepair. In 1973, when the Gregory Melikian family purchased the hotel, it was a flophouse with rooms renting for five dollars a night. The preservation-minded family launched a lengthy restoration project to return the landmark to its status as an elegant hotel.

Under new ownership since 1996, the historic structure continues to "grow into the past" during its present multimillion-dollar restoration. Surrounded by sleek skyscrapers, the gold-toned brick corner structure with bright green canopies no longer ranks as the tallest building in town. But its listing on the National Register of Historic Places testifies to its historical character and architectural quality.

The marble floors in the lobby that wowed guests at the hotel's unveiling seven decades ago are reemerging as the wall-to-wall carpeting which has concealed them for years is removed. From the lobby, romantic arched doorways lead to a charming restaurant specializing in Italian cuisine, and steps descend to an adjacent guest lounge with high ceilings, a skylight, and a raised alcove for cigar smokers.

Upstairs, 132 guest rooms (including 11 suites) have been handsomely refurbished with custom hand-crafted furniture like armoires that conceal televisions, coffee services, and mini-refrigerators. Sedate earth tones of brown, beige, and rust appear in the carpet, bedspreads, and marble-topped desks. The bathrooms feature the original tile floors and pedestal sinks but have been updated with all the modern comforts guests expect of an elegantly restored landmark hotel.

Saguaro Lake Ranch Resort

13020 Bush Highway
Mesa, Arizona 85215
phone: 602-984-2194
fax: 602-380-1490
Steve and Susan Durand, managers

GETTING THERE IS HALF THE FUN when escaping to the Saguaro Lake Ranch Resort. The highway winds along the Salt River through the rugged hills and desert landscape of Tonto National Forest, then surprises travelers with a view of the brilliant blue Saguaro Lake. Rising from the base of a valley are the stark, jagged cliffs of "the Bulldogs"—the local

Saguaro Lake
Ranch Resort

name for the Goldfield Mountains—which are in fact the foothills of the
Superstition Mountains. A road curves sharply off the highway and leads down
to the banks of the Salt River and the Saguaro Lake Ranch Resort.

The ranch began in the late 1920s as a construction site for the crew
building Stewart Mountain Dam, the last in a chain of four dams that
irrigate the valley. The crew's mess hall, built in 1930, is the oldest structure on the site. It serves as the ranch's main lodge today. The structure's
principal attraction stands in the center of the room, a massive four-way
fireplace with raised hearth, built of river rock by a Mexican artisan in
1935. The interesting room also features mounted animal heads, authentic Navajo and Mexican rugs, and a table made from saguaro cactus ribs.

Later, the ranch became a fishing resort and a retreat for alcoholics
who came west to "dry out." It offered modest cabins along the river and
a few up near the lodge, a communal outhouse, a grocery store, an ice-
house, a marina, and a bridge across the river. A flood in 1942 took the
bridge. Six years later, Dottie Kissinger and her husband bought the ranch.

What is now the Bush Highway was a bumpy dirt road when the
Kissingers took over. The buildings' interiors were unfinished, the elec-
tricity was 25-cycle, and the only telephone was the dam's emergency
line. The Kissingers launched a major upgrading project. The original plank
floors were stripped and sanded, wallboard and carpets were installed,

the electrical system was updated, telephone service was added, drapes were made, and chairs were upholstered. In the 1950s, a swimming pool, a shuffleboard court, and a rodeo arena were added.

Still owned by the Kissinger family, the ranch is managed by Dottie's son, Steve Durand, and his wife, Susan. They continue the ranch's long tradition of welcoming back guests from all over the United States and abroad, many of them fourth-generation visitors. Among the many famous people who have stayed here were Norman Rockwell, Mary Martin, Henry Ford III, and Western artist Lon Megargee, whose former home, the Hermosa Inn, is also featured in this book. Movie and television crews find the ranch's setting ideal for Western movies and documentaries.

The guest rooms are in an assortment of cottages with raised, covered porches made from river rock. Each has a modern bathroom and a view of grass, trees, and the stunning "Bulldogs." Five cottages located by the river offer views of the water. As you'd expect in this rugged Western setting, the furnishings are comfortably rustic—simple Monterey oak pieces and hand-painted dressers and headboards.

But you won't be spending much time in your room, because the focus at this ranch is the great outdoors. The Salt River is a favorite among fishermen, tubing enthusiasts, and, when the water is up, rafters. At the corral, guests can preview their mounts for the ranch's breakfast and trail rides. There's a heated swimming pool, croquet on the lawn, a shuffleboard court, a horseshoe area, and plenty of hiking trails in the desert and foothills. Who knows, maybe you'll be the one to discover the Lost Dutchman Mine in the nearby Superstition Mountains.

Rates

The 19 cabins are available to two persons for $110 (American plan) or $85 (breakfast only). A fee is charged for additional persons six years and older. Major credit cards are accepted. No pets are allowed.

San Marcos Resort

One San Marcos Place
Chandler, Arizona 85224
phone: 800-325-3535 or 602-963-6655
fax: 602-899-5441

THE STATE'S FIRST PUBLIC RESORT, the elegant Hotel San Marcos, was built in an isolated farming community southeast of Phoenix in 1912, the same year Arizona achieved statehood. The landmark hotel was the brainchild of wealthy landowner A. J. Chandler, the first veterinary surgeon of the Arizona Territory. His chosen site was the town he founded and which bears his name.

The enterprising doctor hired architect Arthur Benton, an authority on California Mission design, and the finest craftsmen to design and build the resort. An impressive structure of reinforced cast-in-place concrete, arched windows and openings, parapet battlements, and towers with tile roofs, the resort was very progressive for its time and location. Named for Friar Marcos DeNiza, a Spanish explorer said to have visited the area in 1539, the San Marcos opened in 1913 to a crowd of 500 that included the governor of Arizona, Congressman Carl Hayden, and Thomas Marshall,

San Marcos Resort

the vice president of the United States. It offered 35 guest rooms, a spacious lobby, a dining room, a ballroom, retail shops, and administrative offices.

The glamorous San Marcos was the first Arizona resort to offer a 100-acre golf course, tennis, polo, horseback riding, and a constant flow of social activities. News of the luxurious desert retreat spread quickly, and the resort became a favorite playground for screen stars, socialites, industry heads, government officials, and the like. Famous figures who stayed here include President Herbert Hoover, Joan Crawford, Fred Astaire, Gloria Swanson, Margaret Sanger, and Illinois governor Frank O. Lowden, who announced his candidacy for the United States presidency at the San Marcos in 1928.

The legendary resort has undergone expansions throughout its history. By 1932, newspapers reported that the San Marcos could accommodate 225 guests. Dr. Chandler sold the resort in 1937 and was followed by a cast of new owners. When John Quarty, the fourth owner, died in 1979, the guest rooms were closed.

In 1986, a multimillion-dollar expansion and renovation was launched. It resulted in the restoration of the original building, the addition of 250 rooms, and the resurfacing of the romantic pergolas, the vine-covered passageways that frame the historic structure. Listed on the National Register of Historic Places, Arizona's premier winter resort reopened in 1987 as the Sheraton San Marcos. A decade later, the resort awaits further renovation as its new owner, California-based Sunstone Hotel Investors, assumes operations.

The legacy of luxury continues today at the landmark resort, which offers 295 exquisitely furnished guest rooms, a 113-acre golf course, two restaurants, swimming pools, and gift shops. Towering palms, fountains, and flower gardens help preserve the resort's image as an elegant desert oasis. But the spacious 80-year-old lobby—with its arched windows, high ceiling, restored brick fireplace, and adjoining hallway lined with interesting memorabilia—best reflects the illustrious past of the San Marcos.

Rates

The 295 rooms and suites are available for $69 to $305, depending on the season. Special rates that include a full breakfast and two hours of tennis range from $77 to $186.

Amenities

The rooms have private baths, cable television, radios, and telephones with call waiting. Some have balconies or patios. The resort offers a golf course, a bar and grill in the clubhouse, two swimming pools, two restaurants, a nightclub, tennis courts, shops, and an exercise room.

Location

The resort is in the heart of downtown Chandler at the corner of Chandler Boulevard and Arizona Avenue. From Interstate 10, exit onto Chandler Boulevard and travel east to Arizona Avenue.

Noftsger Hill Inn

425 North Street
Globe, Arizona 85501
phone: 520-425-2260
Pamela and Frank Hulme, owners/innkeepers

IT READS "1917 NOFTSGER HILL" above the entrance to this towering

Noftsger Hill Inn

structure, which sits high on a hill overlooking the mining town of Globe. But the inscription tells only half the story. The building actually dates to 1907, when it housed the four-room North Globe Schoolhouse. When the front half of the existing structure was completed in 1917, the name was changed to Noftsger Hill School.

The hill and school were named after Globe businessman A. Noftsger, who once owned the rights to the area's water, which he sold to miners and their families living in the surrounding neighborhoods. Generations of students climbed the hill to attend Noftsger Hill School, among them Rose Mofford, a future governor of Arizona. The school finally closed in 1981. A decade later, it was sold to Pamela and Frank Hulme, who began a renovation project to convert the oversized landmark into a bed-and-breakfast.

It was no easy feat turning the 13,000-square-foot institution into an inviting inn. First, a new roof was installed to stop the rain from running down the stairs. Then the original maple floors and woodwork had to be refinished. The bathrooms needing updating, and the windows and transoms required repair. The tasks seemed endless, but the dedicated owners met the challenge, creating an inn with an atmosphere that is at once grand, gracious, and homelike.

The old school's main hallway now serves as the inn's living room. At 30 by 70 feet, it has plenty of room for the Victorian furnishings, Oriental rugs, and pianos that are arranged into a conversation area. A few steps down the hall in a former classroom is the dining room, where Southwestern-style breakfasts big enough to satisfy a miner are served atop lace-covered antique tables.

Guests are housed in the former classrooms for grades 1, 2, 3, and 4. The enormous rooms have 15-foot ceilings, huge windows, and original slate blackboards, where guests leave comments about their stay. Each has more than one sleeping area and a sitting area grouped around a fireplace. The furnishings include Mission-style and antique pieces, carved armoires, claw-foot tubs, and handmade quilts. The smallest room—formerly the janitor's supply room—has cowboy decor and a cozier feeling. The rooms at the front of the building allow views of the Pinal Mountains, while those in the back face the historic Old Dominion Mine. Old textbooks and a collection of class photos taken during the school's earliest years are on display in a glass cabinet near the main entrance.

Rates

The five rooms are available for $55 to $75. Full breakfast is included. The rooms are wheelchair accessible. Major credit cards are accepted. Smoking is not permitted indoors.

Amenities

All the rooms have private baths, off-street parking, and fireplaces. The larger rooms have sitting areas. The inn offers a common living room and a dining room.

Location

The inn is at the end of North Street. Follow Globe Street north until it becomes North Street. Continue to the top of the hill to the inn.

SOUTHERN ARIZONA

Florence, Safford, Oracle,
Yuma, Ajo, Tucson, Willcox,
Dragoon, Tombstone,
Amado, Tubac/Tumacacori,
Sonoita, Patagonia, Sasabe,
Hereford, Bisbee, Douglas

SOUTHERN ARIZONA spreads across the state with seas of desert and grasslands and mountain ranges that rise over 9,000 feet. Fertile croplands share the countryside with giant saguaros in the Sonoran Desert. Abandoned mines and ghost towns mingle with aged missions and fortresses (presidios) founded in the 1700s by missionaries from Mexico. This is also the former homeland of the feared Chiricahua Apache and their famous warrior chiefs, Cochise and Geronimo.

The land southeast of the Gila River finally joined the United States as part of the New Mexico Territory in 1853 with the signing of the Gadsden Purchase. In 1863, President Abraham Lincoln proclaimed Arizona a separate United States territory.

The area's strong Mexican heritage is still evident in **Tucson**, the state's second-largest city. Tucson is the home of the University of Arizona, founded in 1885. The city's large collection of Mexican restaurants is considered the best in the state. Outside Tucson, the San Xavier del Bac Mission, called the "White Dove of the Desert," still stands on the site selected by Father Eusebio Kino in 1700. This beautiful Moorish-style mission is surrounded by the Tohono O'Odham Indian Reservation, whose residents it serves.

In 1857, Tucson became a stage stop along the Overland Route, offering passengers supplies and protection from Apache attacks. A decade later, it was named the second territorial capital, a title it held for 10 years. Tucson's colorful past included shootouts in the streets, notorious gangsters, and large dude ranches and first-class resorts. Although it has grown into a cosmopolitan city where sleek buildings merge with low, flat-roofed Pueblo-style adobes, Tucson still has a small-town feeling.

Yuma, at the far southwestern corner of the state, began as a gathering point on the Colorado River. Early California gold seekers called it Yuma Crossing. Today, the fertile land is covered with peanut and date farms, citrus groves, vegetable fields, and "snowbirds" in RVs, who overrun the town during Yuma's pleasant winter months.

Crops also prosper in the fertile cattle-ranching country of the Santa Cruz Valley south of Tucson, where the climate is ideal for grape growing. Along the highway in **Sonoita** and **Patagonia**, signs point to vineyards and wineries offering wine-tasting tours and gift shops.

To the southeast, the old silver- and copper-mining towns of **Tombstone** and **Bisbee** make the most of their colorful histories. In Tombstone, "the Town Too Tough to Die," the rootin', tootin' days of the Wild West are replayed every Sunday with the reenactment of the famous 1881 gunfight at the OK Corral. Picturesque Bisbee, which clings to the steep slopes of the Mule Mountains, celebrates its past as a booming copper-mining town by offering travelers an underground tour of its famous mines. The town's well-preserved brick structures line the bottom of a gulch on Main Street in the downtown area known as "Old Bisbee"; many of them house gift shops, cafes, or inns.

Douglas, a tiny town at the far southeastern corner of the state, sits a mile from the Mexican border town of Agua Prieta. The glamorous Gadsden Hotel, a massive five-story structure in the center of town, is its main attraction. Legends and ghost stories keep the past alive in this ornate structure, which still has the nick in its marble staircase reportedly created when the desperado Pancho Villa charged up the steps on horseback in 1912.

Things to do and see

TUCSON AREA

Arizona–Sonoran Desert Museum. This world-famous living museum has animals and plants on display in re-created natural habitats. It is located 14 miles west of Tucson in Tucson Mountain Park. For information, call 520-883-2702.

De Grazia Gallery in the Sun. This is the former home of local artist Ted De Grazia, known for his paintings of Southwestern, Native American, and Mexican life. The museum, a rustic structure built by the artist and friends from materials found in the surrounding desert, features many of De Grazia's original oils, watercolors, and sculptures. A gallery, a chapel, a workshop, and the artist's grave site are also on the grounds. The museum is in northeastern Tucson at 6300 North Swan Road. For information, call 520-299-9191.

El Presidio District. Visitors can take a walking tour of the historic downtown site of the former Spanish fort, the center of activity in Tucson at the turn of the century. Be sure to see the lovely Pima County Courthouse, a domed Spanish Colonial–style structure built in 1927 over the original 1869 adobe courthouse. For information, call the Metropolitan Tucson Convention and Visitors Bureau at 800-638-8350 or 520-624-1817.

Mission San Xavier del Bac. The "White Dove of the Desert," a noteworthy example of Spanish Mission architecture, was established in

1783 by Father Eusebio Kino. The domes, flying buttresses, carvings, and frescoes set it apart from other missions. It is located nine miles south of Tucson on the Tohono O'Odham Indian Reservation. It serves as the tribe's main church. For information, call 520-294-2624.

Old Tucson Studios. Constructed in 1939 by Columbia Pictures, this replica of Tucson in the 1860s was rebuilt and reopened in 1996 after a fire destroyed many of its original structures. Numerous Western films, television series, and commercials have been filmed here. Visitors today can watch live gunfights and Western musical revues and descend into a mine. The studios are in Tucson Mountain Park, 12 miles west of town via Speedway Boulevard or Ajo Way. For information, call 520-883-0100.

TUBAC / TUMACACORI

Tubac. This military garrison, established by the Spanish in 1752, is the state's oldest European settlement. Now a popular art colony with an assortment of galleries, studios, and shops, it is located off Interstate 19 about 45 miles south of Tucson.

Tumacacori National Historical Park. This former Pima Indian village was visited by Father Eusebio Kino in 1691. It is the site of the massive, abandoned Mission San Jose de Tumacacori, built of adobe around 1800. Due to lack of funds, Apache raids, and horrible winter conditions, the mission was abandoned in 1848 and was never completed. The site was named a National Monument in 1908. It is 50 miles south of Tucson off Interstate 19.

Inn at Rancho Sonora

Inn at Rancho Sonora
9198 AZ 79 North
Florence, Arizona 85232
phone: 800-205-6817 or 602-868-8000
Linda and Brent Freeman, owners/innkeepers

THE INN AT RANCHO SONORA is tucked off AZ 79 five miles south of Florence and about 14 miles north of the Tom Mix Monument. The memorial marks the site where Mix, the famous silent-screen cowboy, lost his life in 1940 after crashing his speeding yellow Cord Phantom into the dry desert wash.

You'll know you're almost there when you see a large water tower marked with the letters *RS*. The tower holds water from a 750-foot-deep well and announces the location of the Inn at Rancho Sonora and its sister operation, the Rancho Sonora RV Park. Turn off the highway at the sign and follow the road past saguaros, paloverde trees, coyotes, and quail to a pleasant walled compound.

In the style of the old Spanish missions, the inn and courtyard are enclosed by worn adobe walls made of bricks created from the soil nearby.

Originally, the inn consisted of two adobe structures built in the early 1930s and served as a winter retreat for an affluent family named Evans. Mrs. Evans was known for her gracious hospitality and entertaining and often hosted out-of-town guests at what was then called Rancho Soledad.

Through the years, the ranch fell into neglect and disrepair. In 1993, it was purchased by current owners Linda and Brent Freeman. The Freemans recognized the potential of the 16-acre property for a bed-and-breakfast and a park for recreational vehicles. They immediately began to restore the original ranch, following their goal of preserving its essence while adding the amenities guests expect today. The result is an inviting Southwestern inn centered around a landscaped brick courtyard with an Old World fountain and a comfortable sitting area, a perfect place to enjoy the morning sun and the inn's delicious breakfast pastries.

Guests rooms with names like Delores, Bandito, Alamo, and Evangeline are tastefully furnished with locally handcrafted pieces and decorated according to a variety of themes ranging from rustic cowboy to prim traditional. Although the owners are to be commended for successfully preserving the original concept, guests are happy knowing that each room has a television, a handsome Mission-tile bath, and heating and air conditioning. Elsewhere on the property are three separate fully furnished cottages, an RV park with 65 sites, and a corral for those who want to bring their horses.

Rates

The seven rooms rent for $44 to $64, the three cottages (one bedroom, one bath) for $75 to $85, and the suites (two bedrooms, two baths) for $115 to $125, depending on the season. Rates are negotiable for long stays. Continental breakfast is included. Supervised pets and children are welcome. No smoking is allowed indoors.

Taylor's Bed-and-Breakfast

321 North Bailey Street
Florence, Arizona 85232
phone: 520-868-4857
Eddie Taylor, owner/innkeeper

This tin-roofed adobe inn, which sits on a quiet corner in Florence's historic district, ranks as the best-preserved and least-altered Sonoran-style structure in town. It dates to 1872, when Jesus Martinez, a farmer from New Mexico, began construction on the **U**-shaped structure with a flat dirt roof and a central patio enclosed on three sides. In the mid-1880s, the building was divided into three units to house a residence, a store, and a meat market. A hip roof was added in 1912, and the building was converted into a single residence three years later. The present tin roof was added in the 1960s.

Current owner Eddie Taylor purchased the structure in 1981 and spent a year on its restoration before opening it as a bed-and-breakfast. Taylor made sure his historic structure remained as authentic as today's standards for comfort allowed. Electric lighting and indoor bathrooms have replaced the old gaslights and outdoor privies, but the century-old thick adobe walls and the high saguaro-rib ceilings with their rugged mesquite and pine cross beams are still there.

The owner's large collection of antiques, displayed throughout the inn, spills out into the cement courtyard. It should please history buffs and antique collectors alike. Nearly every antique is for sale, from Victorian gas lamps to antique armoires to rustic wooden wagon wheels salvaged from an old stagecoach. Each of the inn's three guest rooms has a different theme—cowboy, Indian, or Victorian.

In the morning, a hearty home-cooked breakfast is served in the cozy kitchen on an old lion's-paw table or out on the tree-shaded patio.

Rates

The three guest rooms with private baths are available for $49 to $69. Breakfast is included. No pets are allowed. Smoking is not permitted indoors.

Amenities

The inn offers a common living room, a patio with a misting system, and a Jacuzzi. It is within walking distance of downtown Florence's attractions.

Location

The inn is on the southeastern corner of Bailey and Eighth Streets in the historic district of downtown Florence.

Olney House Bed-and-Breakfast

Olney House Bed-and-Breakfast

1104 Central Avenue
Safford, Arizona 85546
phone: 800-814-5118 or 520-428-5118
fax: 520-428-2299
web site: http://www.zekes.com/~olney/
e-mail: olney@zekes.com
Carole and Patrick Mahoney, owners/innkeepers

THE WEST WAS AT ITS WILDEST in the 1870s, when George A. Olney was sheriff of Graham County. Olney earned $2.50 for every arrest. Within two years, the ambitious sheriff collected the staggering sum of $30,000, most of which was used to erect a stately two-story red-brick mansion on a full city block near downtown Safford. Completed in 1890, the 14-room residence featured a Western Colonial Revival–style exterior with a pillared veranda on each level and a sweeping second-floor view of the town, mountain peaks, and the Gila River Valley. The distinguished structure also reflected Olney's former status as a successful cattle rancher, a founding father of Valley National Bank, and a candidate for governor.

Though it no longer occupies an entire city block, the former Olney residence sits on a prominent corner in one of Safford's premier neighborhoods. In 1988, it earned a listing on the National Register of Historic Places and won the hearts of Carole and Patrick Mahoney of San Francisco. After purchasing the sound but neglected structure, the creative couple spent four years restoring it to its turn-of-the-century elegance. The Mahoneys furnished the home with an interesting assortment of antiques and treasures from Southeast Asia and opened it in 1992 as a bed-and-breakfast, the first in Graham County.

Olney would be proud to know that his residence continues to dazzle guests more than a century later. The bright, high-ceilinged rooms feature gleaming original oak and maple floors, oversized windows, 10-foot-tall pocket doors, and distinctive fireplaces inlaid with colorful tiles. To the right of the spacious entrance hall, the former gentlemen's parlor provides a favorite after-breakfast location for guests. These days, ladies who like to linger over a last cup of gourmet coffee following the Mahoneys' morning feast are as welcome as men.

Guests have the run of the entire upper level, which features three inviting bedrooms, a large central bath, and a spacious corner sitting room with a television and a fireplace. The attractively furnished rooms all have corner locations and pleasant views. One features a large bay window, while another opens out to the veranda overlooking the street.

Behind the main house in the shade of an enormous pecan tree are two brick cottages built around 1920, one of them a former summer kitchen. Both offer privacy and amenities that include cable television, kitchenettes, and private baths. The secluded spa tucked between the cottages is just the place to unwind after a day spent sightseeing in the area.

Oracle

Triangle L Ranch

P.O. Box 900
Oracle, Arizona 85623
phone: 520-623-6732 (Tucson) or 520-896-2804 (Oracle)
Tom and Margot Beeston, owners/innkeepers

STACKED-WOOD CORRAL FENCES guide the way to this 80-acre bed-and-breakfast nestled in a secluded valley on the wooded northern slopes of the Santa Catalina Mountains. At the ranch's elevation of 4,500 feet, the air is fresh and smells of pines and junipers. An old windmill turns in the breeze, and huge oak trees tower above the whitewashed adobe dwellings with red tin roofs.

In the 1890s, the ranch was the homestead of William Ladd, a sheep and cattle rancher who used the Triangle L brand for his livestock. Buffalo Bill was a regular guest at the Triangle L, which is considered the first guest ranch in southern Arizona.

The ranch prospered during the early 1920s under the guidance of Mrs. M. J. Tutt. She left in 1924 to oversee the operation of a guest ranch in Dragoon. The Triangle L was sold to a New Yorker and former ranch guest named William Trowbridge, who eventually took an interest in the town of Oracle and endowed it with public buildings. One of the ranch's guest cottages, built by Trowbridge as his personal retreat, features high ceilings, natural lighting, and a large stone fireplace.

The Triangle L continued to run cattle until the 1960s. In 1978, it was sold to Margot and Tom Beeston. The Beestons immediately began restoring the buildings and landscaping the grounds and opened the Triangle L as a bed-and-breakfast. Margot is the ranch cook, landscaper, and licensed wildlife rehabilitator. Tom, the resident handyman and gardener, also makes, restores, and plays stringed musical instruments. You can watch him at work in his studio/shop, located on the grounds.

Guests are accommodated in four carefully restored cottages which date to the turn of the century. One, an ivy-covered cottage with a screened sleeping porch, has a cozy sitting area under shady oaks. Another, a three-bedroom frame cottage, overlooks the ranch and has views of the Santa Catalina Mountains. The cottage with the most secluded setting has a bright, airy interior with an abundance of windows, a screened porch, and a ramada for outside viewing of the desert vistas. The cottages are attractively and comfortably furnished with antique pieces and are separated from each other by footpaths and trees.

Breakfast is served in the roomy kitchen at the main ranch house, where a wood-burning stove removes the winter chill. During the warm months, many guests prefer to dine on the screened back porch or outside on the sunny front porch overlooking a walled iris garden. Morning meals include fresh eggs from the ranch's chickens and Margot's delicious homemade breads and pastries. Entertainment in this tranquil setting is as it was in the old days: reading (or perhaps creating) a masterpiece, hiking, meditating, and napping with neither television nor telephone to distract you.

Rates

The four cottages are available to one or two persons for $65 to $110, depending on the season. The charge for additional guests in the same cottage is $15 per adult and $10 per child. Full breakfast is included. MasterCard, Visa, and Discover are accepted. No pets are allowed. Check-in is after 4 P.M. and check-out at noon.

Amenities

The cottages have private baths. Two have kitchens, one has a fireplace, and two have screened porches. A telephone is in the main ranch building.

Location

The ranch is off AZ 77 about 35 miles northeast of Tucson. From Oracle Junction, follow AZ 77 east for 11 miles. Turn right at the business-loop turnoff into the town of Oracle. Turn left at the Circle K convenience market onto Rockcliff Road. Cross AZ 77 and take the first right turn, onto Oracle Ranch Road. Drive 0.5 mile to Triangle L Ranch Road. The gate is on the left; look for the Triangle L Ranch sign. Close the gate and follow the road to the main ranch house.

Best Western Coronado Motor Hotel

233 4th Avenue
Yuma, Arizona 85364
phone: 800-528-1234 or 520-783-4453
fax: 520-782-7487
Yvonne and John Peach, owners/managers

THE BEST WESTERN CORONADO Motor Hotel, which sprawls for more than a block in the historic district of downtown Yuma, is a treasure chest of area history. It was built by John and Marie Peach, a tailor and his wife from Chicago, who opened their adobe motor hotel in 1938. They named it Casa de Coronado and offered 14 rooms and off-street front-door parking. The guest rooms were located in two side buildings which flanked the Peach family residence. Six years later, 10 rooms and seven garages were added, resulting in a U-shaped structure surrounding the Peach home. The palm trees which tower over the original motel today were planted in 1938 by the Peaches' young son, John, who— with his wife, Yvonne—continues the family tradition as owner and operator today.

Best Western Coronado Motor Hotel

The Coronado's history includes a long list of firsts. It was Yuma's first motor hotel. In 1946, it became one of the first Best Western motor hotels; it remains Best Western's oldest facility. It was also the first motel in town to offer air-conditioned rooms, a fax machine, and VCRs. And in 1911, on a July day in 110-degree heat, the first airplane to land on Arizona soil touched down on the site of the hotel's Yuma Landing Restaurant and Lounge.

A remarkable collection of framed photos, some dating to the beginning of the 20th century, lines the walls of the restaurant and lounge and provides a fascinating peek into Yuma's past. Interesting memorabilia is also on display in the hotel's museum, which occupies the original lobby and the former Peach family residence. The original switchboard is there, along with rooms brimming with items rescued from the family's vast collection—old cash registers, travel guides, kitchenware, and clothing.

Yuma's warm winter temperatures attract hordes of snowbirds, including guests who stayed at the Coronado 40 or 50 years ago. They tell of the days when California had a three-day waiting period between obtaining a marriage license and getting married. Because Arizona had no such wait, many impatient California couples crossed the state line into Yuma to get hitched. Some were Hollywood celebrities, like comedienne Alice Faye, who spent her honeymoon at the Coronado, as did screen cowboy Tom Mix.

Through the years, the motor hotel grew. Today, it spans an entire city block and then some. Fourteen rooms were added to the original property in 1945. In the 1960s, John Peach purchased a motor hotel across the street. He replaced the shake roof with red tile to match the Coronado's and increased his inventory of guest rooms. A 26-room annex was built in 1996, replacing the service station that stood on the corner—the only spot on the block not occupied by the Coronado. When the 25-suite addition currently under construction is completed, the hotel's guest rooms will total 111.

Like it has from the beginning, the Coronado offers guest rooms decorated in a pleasant Southwestern style. The oldest buildings feature original step-down showers, pedestal sinks, and ceramic tiles, which have all held up exceptionally well, due in part to the copper plumbing installed in the 1930s.

Rates

The 86 rooms range in price from $45 for a standard room to $125 for a suite. Weekly and monthly rates are available. Children under 12 are free. No pets are allowed. Credit cards are accepted.

Amenities

The rooms have private baths. Handicapped-accessible rooms are available. The hotel offers two pools, two laundry facilities, an adjacent restaurant and lounge, a museum, cable television, VCRs, and free movies.

Location

The motor hotel is on 4th Avenue in historic downtown Yuma. If you are eastbound on Interstate 8, exit onto 4th Avenue; if you are westbound, take Exit 1 (Giss Parkway) to 4th Avenue.

The Guest House Inn

3 Guest House Road
Ajo, Arizona 85321
phone: 520-387-6133
Norma, Michael, and Chris Walker, owners/innkeepers

LONG BEFORE 1853, when a railroad surveying party discovered Ajo's copper-mining possibilities, the Papago Indians were using the area's abun-

The Guest House Inn

dant copper minerals to paint their bodies. Ajo sounds like the tribe's word for paint, and some say it was thus that the town's name came about. The other version is that Ajo was named for the Spanish word for garlic, which is said to grow in the vicinity.

Although prospectors began settling in the area around the mid-1800s, it wasn't until 1911 that a leaching process made the mining of low-grade ore profitable. The New Cornelia Copper Company (later purchased by Phelps Dodge Corporation) began operations in 1917. The town flourished as a major copper producer under Phelps Dodge until 1985, when mining ceased. Ajo's mile-wide, 1,000-foot-deep open pit mine ranks among the world's largest. It is located just south of town.

When mining operations ended, the town's lifeblood was drained. Homes previously occupied by the families of mine supervisors and workers were put up for sale and were bought up by retirees and snowbirds. One such structure was the Phelps Dodge Guest House, built in 1925 to provide accommodations for visiting mining VIPs. The stately landmark, a bright white frame structure with four columns and a high, peaked roof, was purchased in 1988 by the home's former housekeeper, Norma Walker, and her two sons.

Like most of the structures in this company town, the Southern plantation–style mansion that houses the Guest House Inn was built by Phelps Dodge, which spared no expense in furnishing and maintaining the stately guest quarters. The tradition is continued today by the Walker family, who completely refurbished and renovated the abandoned landmark before opening it to the public as a bed-and-breakfast.

Guests today are given the same VIP treatment that pleased visiting mining officials for more than half a century. Four remodeled guest rooms, each with different decor, feature private baths and French doors that open out to sunny, enclosed side porches. Antique furnishings and brass beds in the Bisbee Room reflect the Victorian era, while the Ajo Room features whitewashed Southwestern decor. The mood in the Old Pueblo Room is Spanish. The Prescott Room's four-poster bed and traditional furnishings bring back Arizona's territorial days.

The elegant common room has sofas flanking the fireplace and the television. It is a comfortable place for guests to gather after a day of sightseeing. The stately rear dining room, with its wall of windows and handsome 20-foot walnut dining table made by local craftsmen, is the perfect setting for one of Norma Walker's sumptuous breakfasts.

Rates

The four rooms are available for $79. Full breakfast is included. MasterCard, Visa, Diners Club, and American Express are accepted. Smoking is not permitted. No pets are allowed.

Amenities

Three of the guest rooms have queen-size beds, and one has twin beds. All have private baths and individual cooling and heating controls. The inn offers a television, a telephone, and a fireplace in the common room.

Location

*Ajo is 108 miles south of Phoenix and 130 miles west of Tucson on AZ 85. Turn south at the stoplight onto La Mina Avenue and follow the signs to Guest House Road.
The inn is at the end of the street.*

The Mine Manager's House Inn

The Mine Manager's House Inn
I Greenway Drive
Ajo, Arizona 85321
phone: 520-387-6505
fax: 520-387-6508
Micheline and Jean Fournier, owners/innkeepers

AJO'S GIANT OPEN-PIT COPPER MINE, which supported the town's citizens for more than a half-century, required someone with a sharp eye to oversee day-to-day operations. The New Cornelia Mining Company made the job easier by providing its key man and his family with a handsome residence atop the town's highest hill. From this lofty perch, the mine manager could see for 30 miles and keep a watchful eye on the entire town, day and night.

The manager's residence was constructed in 1919 of solid masonry. Its 10-inch-thick walls were designed to withstand the constant blasting from the nearby mine. The booming continued for seven decades, and through it all, the house on the hill provided comfortable living quarters for each of the mine's 12 managers. The first, Michael Curley, occupied the home until his retirement in 1939. Through the years, rooms were added to the structure as managers and their families came and went. Eventually, the home grew to its present size of 5,000 square feet.

When mining operations ceased in 1985, the empty manager's house was put up for sale. It was purchased by an enterprising couple named

Jeffries, who converted it and the surrounding three acres of terraced gardens into a splendid bed-and-breakfast. In 1990, the inn was sold to Micheline and Jean Fournier, a gracious French Canadian couple from California. Now, it's the Fourniers and their guests who overlook the town from the handsome hilltop house.

A large world map behind the reception desk marks the origins of guests, who have traveled from as far away as Mongolia to experience the inn's hospitality. And it's no wonder. With five appealing guest rooms, gathering areas both indoors and out, a hot tub and spa, and the best view in town, the historic house is worth the trip. Each guest room, decorated in a different motif, features high ceilings and a private bath. The most luxurious, the Greenway Suite, has a romantic Southwestern flavor and features a sitting area and a marble bathtub. It was named after John Greenway, the mining engineer who in 1916 laid out the town of Ajo; he was buried here in 1926. Other guest rooms include the Nautical Room, which has a 180-degree view of the town and is wheelchair accessible, and the Quito Baquito Suite, which features a cozy sitting room and a separate bedroom.

A full breakfast is served in the sunny dining room on the pecan table made for the mining company in the 1920s. Micheline's specialties—Belgian Waffles and Eggs Benedict—are elegantly served on fine china in a room whose splendid view provides an excuse to linger over a last cup of gourmet coffee. A back patio with an adjacent hot tub is designed exclusively for guests' use. It has a refrigerator stocked with cold drinks and a serving bar which was once Ajo's first church altar.

Rates

The two double rooms and three suites are available for $69 to $99. Full breakfast is included. Visa and MasterCard are accepted. Pets are not allowed. No smoking is permitted indoors.

Amenities

The rooms have private baths and telephones. A television and a VCR are in the living room. The inn offers a library, a coin laundry, an outdoor hot tub, and lighted off-street parking.

Location

The inn is on Greenway Drive. From AZ 85 in downtown Ajo, turn south at the stoplight across from the plaza. Travel four blocks, then bear right at the Mine Manager's House sign. Follow the winding road to the inn, located at the top of the hill.

Adobe Rose Inn Bed-and-Breakfast

940 North Olsen Avenue
Tucson, Arizona 85719
phone: 800-328-4122 or 520-318-4644
fax: 520-325-0055
Diana Graham, innkeeper

LOCATED ON A QUIET CORNER two blocks from the University of Arizona, the Adobe Rose Inn is a favorite stopover for visiting faculty, out-of-town parents, and faithful alumni who come to cheer for their beloved Wildcats at the nearby UA stadium. As its name implies, the inn is a pink stucco Pueblo-style structure. It was built in 1933 in a historic neighborhood named after one of Tucson's pioneers and civic leaders. Sam Hughes, a Welsh-born merchant and cattleman, settled in Tucson in the 1850s and later became a business and political leader. Although Hughes lacked a formal education, he was instrumental in establishing

Adobe Rose Inn Bed-and-Breakfast

the city's public-school system. The Adobe Rose Inn is located near the elementary school named in his honor.

Privacy reigns behind the iron gates and six-foot walls that surround the inn's property. Inside, all is tranquil thanks to the adobe walls, which are over a foot thick, and a bougainvillea-draped pool area that beckons like a desert sanctuary. It's hard to believe that this inviting inn is only two blocks from the UA campus and a short walk from the area's assorted shops, eateries, and trendy coffee houses.

The inn offers three attractively furnished bedrooms in the main residence and two unattached cottages suitable for extended stays. All rooms have private baths and cable television; some have private entrances. The casual, comfortable Southwestern style is reflected throughout in the lodgepole-pine furnishings, the gleaming original oak floors, the hand-painted Mexican tiles, and the stained-glass windows.

If a university area doesn't seem like an ideal escape site, think again. The historically significant University of Arizona, founded in 1891, sprawls across 325 acres and offers a host of museums to please even the most discriminating stargazer, artist, photographer, or history buff. Tucked inside the university's main gate is the Arizona State Museum, the state's oldest. It houses a variety of displays that explore Arizona's ancient history and traditions.

Tucson's clear desert night skies make it a major center for astronomy. The Grace H. Flandrau Science Center and Planetarium, located in the university district within walking distance of the inn, features a 16-inch public telescope, a rock-and-gem collection, and laser light shows.

Guests will enjoy the inn's satisfying breakfasts, which feature a variety of gourmet items and are served family-style in the dining room. The inn's kitchen makes every effort to accommodate guests' dietary requirements.

Rates

The three rooms and two cottages are available for $55 to $115, depending on the season and the room. Breakfast is included. Check-in is from 3 P.M. to 6 P.M. and check-out at 11 A.M.

Amenities

All rooms have private baths and cable television. The inn offers a pool, a patio, and a common living room with a fireplace. Children and pets are not allowed. Smoking is not permitted.

Location

The inn is at the corner of North Olsen Avenue and East Second Street. It is two blocks east of Campbell Avenue and the eastern entrance to the University of Arizona.

Arizona Inn

2200 East Elm Street
Tucson, Arizona 85719
phone: 800-678-8946 or 520-325-1541
fax: 520-881-5830

THE ARIZONA INN was an isolated desert retreat far from downtown Tucson when it opened in 1930. Today, more than six decades later, the

Arizona Inn

venerable resort sits in the middle of a residential neighborhood in the city's midtown area, a block or two from the University of Arizona Medical Center. The fact that the town's sprawl has enclosed the inn hasn't changed the luxurious feeling of seclusion that still exists at this cloistered 14-acre retreat, considered one of the Southwest's most elegant hideaways. That, of course, is just the way Isabella Greenway planned it.

Greenway, the human dynamo who created the resort, was a wealthy socialite, Arizona's first congresswoman, and a shrewd businesswoman. Her purpose in founding the inn was twofold. She wanted to create a private winter refuge for her well-heeled friends, many of whom were celebrities or dignitaries. (Isabella was one of Eleanor Roosevelt's brides-maids, and President Theodore Roosevelt attended Isabella's wedding.) She also wanted to establish a customer base for her furniture factory, which employed World War I veterans recuperating from illness in the arid desert. Many handcrafted pieces from the factory are in use today at the inn.

The sprawling stucco inn is painted the same vibrant coral pink and trimmed in the same blue Greenway selected in the 1930s. The 80 spacious, comfortable rooms provide guests with maximum privacy, restful decor, private baths, air conditioning, and color televisions. Many rooms offer a view of the manicured lawns, the lush flower gardens, the fountains, and the winding walkways that have made this lovely inn, listed on the National Register of Historic Places, a favorite for weddings and return vacations by winter visitors.

Although the inn is Tucson's oldest resort and reflects the continuity of 65-plus years of family ownership, it also offers the modern comforts found in most major resorts. Guests can lounge beside a sheltered, 60-foot heated pool, play tennis on clay courts, and select a book from the main sitting room's well-stocked library corner. The award-winning cuisine is served indoors and out in the inn's three dining rooms. The dome-ceilinged cocktail lounge features an impressive collection of Audubons and a pianist who entertains nightly.

The inn's convenience to the airport, the University of Arizona and its medical center, and downtown makes it a popular retreat for celebrities and government officials. But you'd never know, because the tradition established by Isabella Greenway many years ago of never exploiting a guest's celebrity status is still honored at the historic Arizona Inn.

Rates

The inn offers 80 rooms. Singles and doubles are available for $87 to $226 and suites for $110 to $495, depending on the season. The inn is open all year. Children are welcome, but pets are not allowed.

Amenities

All rooms have private baths and color televisions; some have fireplaces and private patios. The inn offers a swimming pool, three restaurants, a lounge, a library, tennis courts, and gardens.

Location

The inn is on East Elm Street two blocks east of Campbell Avenue, between Speedway Boulevard and Grant Road.

Casa Alegre Bed-and-Breakfast Inn

Casa Alegre Bed-and-Breakfast Inn

316 East Speedway Boulevard
Tucson, Arizona 85705
phone: 800-628-5654 or 520-628-1800
fax: 520-792-1880
Phyllis Florek, owner/innkeeper

FOR INNKEEPER PHYLLIS FLOREK, deciding on a name for her bed-and-breakfast was easy. She sensed during her first visit to the old Craftsman bungalow on Speedway Boulevard that it was occupied by happy spirits. Thus the name Casa Alegre, which means "happy house" in Spanish.

The one-story structure, built of double bricks faced with cement stucco, was constructed in 1915 on a lava-rock foundation. Designed as a two-bedroom home, it was the residence of a pharmacist, who lived in the home for 25 years and added rooms as his family grew. The next owner, a physician, practiced in the front bedrooms of the home; his living room doubled as an office and waiting room. After standing vacant for five years, the house was purchased in 1990 by Florek, who spent two years renovating and landscaping before she opened her cozy, comfortable bed-and-breakfast.

A rugged fireplace of volcanic stone is the focal point of the Victorian living room and the dining room, which feature Oriental rugs, original hardwood floors, and mahogany and leaded-glass built-in cabinetry. The sunny, brick-floored Arizona Room, once an open front porch, has been converted into a cozy den where guests can gather after a day of sightseeing to watch television or a movie on the VCR.

In 1994, Florek purchased the one-story 1923 bungalow next door and added it to the inn. The result is a sprawling complex of three double rooms with private baths and a suite with two bedrooms and a kitchen. The innkeeper's collection of antiques and unique pieces decorates the guest rooms and reflects Tucson's heritage. The rustic Hacienda Room features hand-carved furniture from Mexico. The Saguaro Room has a fireplace, a lodgepole-pine bed, and curtain rods made from saguaro ribs.

The inn offers a swimming pool and well-tended gardens filled with cactuses, flowering annuals, and citrus trees. The hot tub, tucked behind a vine-covered partition, is a wonderful place to relax at the end of the day. Tiny lights twinkle in the evenings on the covered backyard patio, which is also a choice spot for breakfast on sunny mornings.

Casa Alegre is conveniently located in the historic West University neighborhood within walking distance of the University of Arizona and its eclectic Fourth Avenue shops.

Rates

The four rooms (including a two-bedroom suite) are available for $70 to $95. Breakfast is included. Well-behaved children are welcome, but pets are not. Smoking is permitted outdoors only. Check-in is from 4 P.M. to 7 P.M. and check-out at noon.

Amenities

All the rooms have private baths. The inn offers private off-street parking. A telephone, a television, and a VCR are in the Arizona Room.

Location

From Interstate 10, exit at Speedway Boulevard. Drive east for one mile. The inn is on the southeastern corner of Speedway Boulevard and Fifth Avenue.

Catalina Park Inn

Catalina Park Inn
309 East 1st Street
Tucson, Arizona 85705
phone: 800-792-4885 or 520-792-4541
fax: 520-792-0838
Mark Hall and Paul Richard, owners/innkeepers

THE STATELY NEOCLASSICAL two-story structure that houses the Catalina Park Inn seems perfectly suited for its role as a bed-and-breakfast. Its corner location on two city lots across the street from Catalina Park in one of Tucson's historic residential neighborhoods definitely adds to its charm. Back in 1993, such were the thoughts running through the heads of Paul Richard and Mark Hall, two house-hunting San Franciscans, when they visited the structure, which appeared as a sorority house in the movie *Revenge of the Nerds*.

The 4,300-square-foot stucco home with columns flanking the entrance was built in 1927 for Harry E. Holbert, a banker who served on the city council, and his wife, Edith, a designer of women's rattlesnake-skin clothing. Shortly after construction, a family from the East named Ivins moved in; the family occupied the home until 1978. Although the property has changed hands a total of eight times, each owner has maintained the structure well. The home's airy rooms and quality craftsmanship, evident in the original Mexican mahogany molding, gleaming oak floors, and paneled staircase, impressed Hall and Richard, who dreamed of owning and operating a bed-and-breakfast. Their bid was accepted and a new business launched.

To ready the inn for guests, the partners pooled their training in interior design, cooking, and landscaping and spent months painting, planting, decorating, and furnishing the structure with their seven-ton collection of thrift-shop antiques. Eclectic treasures abound in a refined, tranquil atmosphere. Soft classical music drifts through the rooms on the main level. In the dining room, walls painted a bold tomato-soup red provide a dramatic backdrop for the owners' interesting artwork. An old butler's pantry near the kitchen serves as a coffee-and-tea bar for guests. Upstairs, there's a four-poster "cannonball" bed and a bathroom with an original Art Nouveau border.

The inn offers four comfortable guest rooms. Three are on the second floor and the fourth is a detached cottage which once served as the servant's quarters. All have private baths, and two of the upstairs rooms feature balconies with park or mountain views for those who would like to enjoy Tucson's spectacular sunsets and sunrises. The colorful cottage features Mexican folk-art pieces, a private garden, and a covered terrace. The landscaped grounds surrounding the home have been given as much attention as the interior. Twin side porches allow a view of the rose garden, which contains at least 30 varieties of roses.

The delicious breakfasts are, as you prefer, served in the dining room or the breakfast room or are delivered to your door with the morning newspaper. Consider yourself blessed if Mark Hall's yummy Papaya and Lime Scones are on the menu.

Rates

The four rooms with private baths range from $90 to $130, based on single or double occupancy. Children over 10 years of age are welcome. No pets are allowed. Smoking is not permitted indoors. Visa, MasterCard, and checks are accepted.

Copper Bell Bed-and-Breakfast

**25 North Westmoreland Avenue
Tucson, Arizona 85745
phone: 520-629-9229
Gertrude and Hans Herbert Kraus, innkeepers**

ONCE UPON A TIME, Sentinel Peak, a small mountain just west of downtown Tucson, was a lookout point for hostile Indians. There was no big white *A* on its face then like there is today. The giant letter became a tradition in 1915 after a University of Arizona football victory. Now, UA freshmen whitewash the giant *A* every year while enjoying a panoramic view of the sprawling city.

The unusual Copper Bell Bed-and-Breakfast is located at the base of Sentinel Peak in the Menlo Park neighborhood. The house, built of lava rock reportedly hauled from the nearby Tohono O'Odham Indian Reservation, was designed by Henry O. Jaastad in a combination of architectural styles. Construction began on the formidable two-story structure in 1907 and was completed by builder L. J. Boudreaux in 1920. Considered an area landmark and known as "Las Piedras" (Spanish for "The

Copper Bell Bed-and-Breakfast

Rocks"), the residence's rugged facade makes an imposing impression in a neighborhood of modest single-level structures.

When Gertrude and Hans Herbert Kraus spotted the rock house in 1989, the vacationing couple knew it had found the aged, solid gem it was seeking, the one that would prompt a relocation from Hamburg, Germany, to Tucson. Because the house had been vacant for a few years except for occasional transients, the Krauses knew that restoring the tarnished jewel would take hard work. That it did. The year of labor included gutting the decayed interior, restoring the original oak floors, and adding tiled baths. Before opening their home as a bed-and-breakfast, the Krauses filled it with several tons of furnishings brought from their homeland.

The inn is named after the old copper bell, brought from a German church, that hangs in an archway on the front porch. The double mahogany front doors, also transported from Germany, contain 48 panes of concave glass. Inside the inn are bright, immaculate rooms filled with German heirlooms including doors, windows, building materials, and linens. Gertrude's stained-glass work appears throughout the house and is most noticeable in the sun-filled dining room, where hearty German breakfasts are served. Everything is made from scratch, with Gertrude's resident chicken providing fresh eggs.

The inn, listed on the National Register of Historic Places, offers six individually decorated guest rooms featuring handmade quilts and stained-glass windows. Three rooms are in the main house, and the others are in a separate guesthouse at the rear of the property. Each room in the rear guesthouse has a private bath and ground-level entry. The spacious Arizona Room, in an upstairs corner of the main house, has a private balcony and a view of the city. The cozy fireplace in the main living room is a popular place for guests to gather for warmth and conversation after seeing the historical sites in the Tucson area.

Rates

From May 1 to August 31, the rooms are available for $55 and up. From September 1 to April 30, they are available for $75 and up. Breakfast is included. Personal checks, traveler's checks, and cash are accepted, but credit cards are not. A two-night minimum stay is required. Children are welcome, but pets are not allowed.

Amenities

Four of the six rooms have private baths, and the remaining two share a bath. The inn offers a front porch, a cactus garden, and a dining room. Smoking is restricted to the patio and garden areas.

Location

From Interstate 10, take Exit 258 (Broadway-Congress). Follow Congress Street to Westmoreland Avenue. Turn right. The Copper Bell is the first house on the left.

El Presidio Bed-and-Breakfast Inn

297 North Main Street
Tucson, Arizona 85701
phone: 800-349-6151 or 520-623-6151
Jerry Toci, owner/innkeeper

THE DISTINGUISHED-LOOKING STRUCTURE that houses El Presidio Bed-and-Breakfast Inn barely resembles its humble beginnings. The home

El Presidio Bed-and-Breakfast Inn

was built in 1876 as a modest, square, flat-roofed adobe. Its location on Main Street near the presidio, the outpost established by the Spanish in 1775, gave the house an air of distinction. Changes were made to the house after the railroad came to town in 1880, when many Main Street residences were enhanced with elegant Victorian touches.

By the time railroad heir Julius Kruttschnitt arrived in Tucson in 1912, the adobe structure on Main Street had been handsomely updated with a hip roof, a graceful veranda, and a balustrade. It was the right home in the right neighborhood. Kruttschnitt purchased it and became an active member of Tucson's social set, many of whom shared Main Street addresses in "Snob Hollow." As the years went by, in-town residents gradually migrated to the sprawling suburbs. The elegant Kruttschnitt House was converted into apartments, its courtyard paved over and its veranda removed.

In 1975, husband-and-wife team Jerry and Patti Toci purchased the home and began a painstaking restoration project that took 10 years. They made many trips to Mexico to find master craftsmen to restore the home's authentic but crumbling adobe walls. Cobblestone and brick walkways were laid, and gardens were planted with flowers and shrubs popular back in the 1880s. Finally, in 1987, with treasures from their extensive collection of antiques in place, the Tocis opened the three beautifully furnished suites of their El Presidio Bed-and-Breakfast Inn.

The main house follows the traditional adobe pattern, with rooms flowing from a *zaguan*, a wide hallway with 17-foot ceilings and walls 21 inches thick. Today, the living room occupies the former *zaguan*. It contains an eclectic merging of antiques ranging from ancient Indian baskets to a 17th-century grandfather clock. The suites feature individual decor and provide guests with a maximum of privacy. The Victorian Suite has a sitting room with white wicker furniture gathered around a kiva fireplace. The other two suites have garden entrances and courtyard views.

In the tradition of the early settlers, the owners restored the courtyard to reflect its importance as the heart of family life—a place to find respite from the heat, to work, to play, to cook, and to sleep. Early courtyards often included a garden and a bubbling fountain, like the three-tiered fountain from Mexico that the owners had dismantled and carted to Tucson in a rickety produce truck. Although air conditioning and a host of other modern amenities have been added to the historic structure, the courtyard—with its high, thick walls and massive gates—remains an important extension of the house. It makes a delightful backdrop during breakfast, an elaborate affair served in an airy room overlooking the courtyard.

Rates

The three suites with private baths are available for $95 to $115. Full breakfast is included. Cash and checks are accepted, but credit cards are not.

Amenities

Televisions, phones, and bathrobes are in each room. Two of the suites have kitchens. The inn offers a garden and a courtyard. It is within walking distance of restaurants, shops, museums, and art galleries.

Location

The inn is east of Interstate 10 at the corner of Main and Franklin Streets in historic downtown Tucson.

Elysian Grove Market Bed-and-Breakfast Inn

Elysian Grove Market
Bed-and-Breakfast Inn

400 West Simpson Street
Tucson, Arizona 85701
phone: 520-628-1522
Deborah LaChapelle, owner/innkeeper

BELIEVE IT OR NOT, once upon a time in downtown Tucson, there was an eight-acre resort where roses and fruit trees lined the banks of lakes. It was called Carrillo's Garden, after entrepreneur Leopoldo Carrillo, who developed the resort park in the 1880s. In 1903, the park became known as Elysian Grove after it was purchased by Emanuel Drachman, who added a pavilion featuring live entertainment, Arizona's first dog races, and outdoor movies. The fun and games came to an end in 1915, when the park was sold for residential use and became the site of an intermediate school. Adobe homes began to appear on the narrow streets, and the Barrio Elysian Grove, also known as "El Hoyo," was born.

In 1924, Jose Trujillo built a market in the barrio, using adobe bricks made on the site. As time went on, more rooms and a basement were added. Trujillo became a popular member of the community, prized for his Mexican sausage, called chorizo, and his practice of accepting pigs, produce, and other items in trade. Stories of Trujillo's backyard bistro and dancing bear are still told by longtime neighbors.

The market was sold in the 1960s and deteriorated into a series of rundown apartments until Californian Debbie LaChapelle spotted the old adobe complex with the words *Elysian Grove Market* over its front doors. LaChapelle recognized the potential in the dilapidated, thick-walled former grocery store and became its third owner.

It took her eight years of tiling bathrooms, retexturing walls, and hand-stripping 40 years' worth of paint off the market's front double doors before the inn was ready for business. A kitchen was constructed in the old market's meat locker, using the locker's 12-inch-thick fuchsia doors. The colorful room appeared in the movie *Boys on the Side*, starring Whoopi Goldberg, who moved into the apartment as part of the story line.

The inn offers four guest rooms or two separate two-level suites, each with a sitting area, a fireplace, a Mexican-tile bath, and a ground-floor exit to the backyard garden. The furnishings are an eclectic mixture of Native American and Mexican styles. Old oak floors gleam under 12- to 16-foot-high ceilings. Wherever you turn, there's something interesting to see: hammered tin pieces, Navajo rugs, and work by local artists. In the spacious enclosed backyard, aged mesquite and tamarisk trees provide a leafy canopy over roof-high prickly-pear cactuses and conversation areas. The parklike setting is a perfect place to linger over a last cup of Colombian coffee after devouring one of Debbie's Mexican-style breakfasts.

Rates

The four rooms, which share two baths and two sitting areas, are available for $75. Or two two-bedroom suites (one with a kitchen) can be rented for $150. Credit cards are not accepted. No pets are allowed.

Hacienda del Sol Guest Ranch Resort

5601 North Hacienda del Sol Road
Tucson, Arizona 85718
phone: 800-728-6514 or 520-299-1501

THE HACIENDA DEL SOL, a romantic adobe structure, spreads across the highest ridge of the Santa Catalina foothills north of Tucson. Built in 1929 as a nondenominational prep school for girls, it was designed in the Spanish-Mexican style by Tucson's famous architect of the day, Josias T. Joesler. The school appealed to the elite and was able to operate with a small enrollment until World War II approached. Classes came to a halt when it became impossible to maintain a proper teaching staff.

After the war, the structure was converted and expanded into a guest ranch. From the late 1950s until 1970, it operated as an exclusive private club, claiming members from around the country and abroad. Through the years, the "Home of the Sun" has hosted many distinguished guests, among them the Westinghouse family, the king of Finland, Spencer Tracy, Katharine Hepburn, and Clark Gable. In 1983, it was reopened to the

Hacienda del Sol Guest Ranch Resort

public as a guest ranch in a lush, 34-acre desert setting where daylight brings spectacular mountain views and nighttime brings star-filled skies and the twinkling lights of Tucson in the distance.

An Old World elegance exists throughout the hacienda. You'll feel it as soon as you pass through the carved wooden gates into the landscaped courtyard. Pathways head in all directions. One leads to the former school's dining hall, now a gourmet restaurant with sweeping desert and mountain views. Another leads to the pool and the Casa Feliz (the "Merry House"), a social center for guests. The path to the right takes you to the main lobby, where the focal point is an old adobe fireplace with distinctive scrollwork and surrounding thick adobe walls. Just beyond the lobby is the original library, where aged, well-stocked bookcases hold a unique collection of recent books as well as the school's dictionary, which dates to 1929.

The original schoolrooms and dormitory are located along a glass-enclosed hallway with gleaming tile floors and authentic period furnishings. Former students return occasionally to request their old rooms. They find the rooms creatively enhanced by vivid colors and attractive Mexican handcrafted furniture. The Spanish-Mexican decor throughout the Hacienda del Sol features carved period pieces and regional folk art reflecting the structure's original design. The headmistress's suite at the rear of the courtyard has dramatic deep green walls, a cozy sitting room, a colorful blue-and-white-tiled bath, and pierced-tin lampshades and mirror frames. Sliding doors open out to a walled patio which is surrounded by cactus gardens and offers a view of the city.

Across the property, casitas—built later with private patios, roomy closets, and spacious baths—cluster around landscaped lawns and flower beds. It's no wonder that this serene desert retreat is a favorite of honeymooners and stressed-out executives seeking to rejuvenate their spirits.

Rates

The 46 rooms are available for $70 to $285, depending on the size of the room and the season. Breakfast is included. Children are welcome. Pets are allowed with an advance deposit. The resort is open all year. Major credit cards are accepted.

Amenities

The rooms have twin, double, queen-, or king-size beds. Some have fireplaces and kitchenettes. All have private baths and telephones. The resort offers a swimming pool, a spa, a library, a tennis court, walking paths, horseback riding, yoga, massages, wheelchair access, and conference facilities. World-class golf is available nearby.

Location

The resort is approximately two miles north of River Road off Hacienda del Sol Road. Follow the signs.

Hotel Congress

311 East Congress Street
Tucson, Arizona 85701
phone: 800-722-8848 or 520-622-8848
fax: 520-792-6366

THE HISTORIC HOTEL CONGRESS, which takes up an entire triangular city block in downtown Tucson, was built in 1919 during the heyday of train travel. The impressive brick-and-marble structure was erected primarily to serve Southern Pacific Railroad passengers, who arrived and departed from the train depot across the street. But it didn't take long for locals to discover the hotel's rollicking Tap Room, which became a favorite hangout for the town's movers and shakers during the "Flapper Era" of the 1920s and 1930s.

The Hotel Congress also attracted gangsters looking for a place to "hole up," which is just what notorious outlaw John Dillinger and his gang did on a fateful night in January 1934. The raging fire that swept the top floor of the three-story hotel that night eventually led to the capture of Dillinger and his companions, all members of the FBI's most wanted list. The firemen who rescued the gangsters and their heavy bags (which concealed machine guns, bullet-proof vests, and $6,000) recognized the famous faces from FBI mug shots and tipped off the local police. A few days later, the gangsters were behind bars, outwitted and captured by Tucson police. Dillinger was extradited to Chicago, where he was later gunned down after a prison escape.

The fire-gutted third floor was never restored, so the hotel became a two-story building with 40 guest rooms on the second floor. The lobby, the adjoining Tap Room, a cafe, a nightclub, and gift shops occupy the first level. The original Southwestern Art Deco style is reflected in the colorful lobby, which features walls painted with Indian designs, the work of a local artist. The hotel's original safe and a collection of framed photos portraying Tucson at an earlier time are located near the reception counter. Old-fashioned phone booths with glass doors remind guests of the days when public-telephone conversations were private matters.

Aged hotels require constant maintenance. Renovation is an ongoing process at this last of the grand, old downtown hotels, where history buffs will enjoy the chance to steep themselves in the flavor of a bygone era. The guest rooms vary in size, but all feature the hotel's original iron beds and black-and-white-tiled baths. Other items sure to touch off a wave of nostalgia include leaded-glass transoms and 1940s-style cabinet radios.

Hotel Congress

The hotel's convenient location across the street from the Amtrak and Greyhound terminals makes it a favorite with budget-minded travelers, including touring European and Japanese students looking for a clean, low-cost hostel. At the Hotel Congress, they enjoy rock-bottom rates, especially for rooms located above the noisy nightclub, the hotel's former dining room. Guests desiring quieter quarters should ask for a room on the western side of the building.

Rates

The 40 renovated rooms are available for $42 to $55 from December to April and $29 to $45 from May to November. Discounts are offered for seniors and students. Major credit cards are accepted.

Amenities

The rooms have baths, telephones, and radios. The hotel offers a cafe, a hair salon, a bar, and a nightclub. The downtown location is within walking distance of shops, galleries, restaurants, and the train and bus stations.

Location

The hotel takes up a full block in downtown Tucson. The main entrance is on East Congress Street between Fourth and Fifth Avenues. The rear entrance and parking are on Toole Avenue.

La Posada del Valle

La Posada del Valle

1640 North Campbell Avenue
Tucson, Arizona 85719
phone and fax: 520-795-3840
Karin Dennen, owner/innkeeper

THE PINK ADOBE-AND-STUCCO structure that houses La Posada del Valle ("The Inn of the Valley") was designed by Josias Joesler, a celebrated Swiss architect known for his ability to combine timeless antiquity with avant-garde style. Joesler designed a number of prominent structures in Tucson in the combined Spanish Colonial–Territorial style, using arches, breezeways, and patios to represent the outdoor lifestyle enjoyed in desert climates. La Posada del Valle is a gracious example of Joesler's early Sante Fe design, which has since been adapted by other Southwestern architects.

In 1929, when the low-slung adobe structure was built as an elegant private residence, the surrounding desert was considered the outskirts of the city. Today, the historic inn, which opened in 1987 and claims to be Tucson's first bed-and-breakfast, is situated in a quiet, respectable neighborhood in the city's midtown area across the street from the University of Arizona Medical Center and a few blocks away from the UA campus. An unassuming pink-walled exterior disguises a refreshing, eclectic interior. The inn offers relaxing patios and landscaped gardens shaded by citrus trees and bursting with colorful bougainvillea, pansies, and bulbs.

Innkeeper Karin Dennen, originally from South Africa, has kept the architect's Southwestern inspiration alive by combining various furniture styles with interesting antiques. The inviting, light-filled living room, where tea is served in the afternoon, features an adobe fireplace with a copper hood and floor-to-ceiling bookcases brimming with interesting books about the Southwest. A collection of framed Walter Keene prints featuring large-eyed children and a striking oil painting of a Latin beauty clenching a rose in her teeth add a touch of drama to the room. The adjoining dining room offers a picture-window view of the Santa Catalina Mountains, which make a perfect backdrop for the gourmet breakfasts. Adding to the inn's charm are the South African treasures the owner has cleverly incorporated into the decor. Handmade baskets and other objects fill the shelves on the airy sun porch.

Guests are accommodated in two sizable suites and three spacious rooms, all with private baths and outside entrances. The rooms are named for (and decorated in honor of) famous women of the 1920s and 1930s. Sophie's Room, named for stage star Sophie Tucker, features an 1818 king-size bed smothered with fluffy eyelet-trimmed pillows, a chaise lounge, an antique dressing table, and a feather boa draped over a mirror. Other rooms honor Isadora Duncan, Pola Negri, and Claudette Colbert. The charming detached cottage at the rear of the courtyard, named for writer Karen Blixen, features early 1900s African furnishings.

The inn's location makes it convenient to Tucson's many attractions. The intimate walled courtyard, surrounded by landscaped gardens and scented by the sweet aroma of orange blossoms, is the ideal spot for unwinding and enjoying the city's relaxed pace and sunny climate. German-speaking guests should be happy to know that Deutsch is spoken at the inn.

Rates

The five rooms (including one cottage with a kitchenette) are available for $90 to $125. During high season, which runs from January 15 to March 31, add $10 per room. Gourmet breakfast and afternoon tea are included. Visa, MasterCard, and personal checks are accepted. Children (particularly those over age 12) are welcome. No pets are allowed. Smoking is not permitted.

Amenities

The rooms have private baths; two rooms have phones. Televisions are in the living room and the cottage. The inn offers a walled courtyard. La Posada del Valle is across the street from the University of Arizona Medical Center and is within walking distance of the UA campus. German is spoken.

Location

From Interstate 10, exit at Speedway Boulevard. Travel east on Speedway to Campbell Avenue and turn left. Follow Campbell north to Elm Street. Turn right on Elm and enter the inn's guest parking, on the right.

Lazy K Bar Guest Ranch

8401 North Scenic Drive
Tucson, Arizona 85743
phone: 520-744-3050
Carol Moore, general manager

THE NEXT TIME you come across an old Western, look closely, because it might have been filmed at the Lazy K Bar Guest Ranch. Audie Murphy, Joseph Cotten, and Robert Wagner were a few of the stars who made films at this picturesque ranch nestled at the base of the Tucson Mountains 16 miles northwest of Tucson.

Lazy K Bar Guest Ranch

The story of the Lazy K Bar Guest Ranch began in 1936, when the 160-acre homestead of Elmer A. Staggs was purchased by a family from Montana named Van Cline. The homestead included an adobe house built in 1933 which still stands today. The Van Clines, who also owned a summer operation in Montana, added a lobby, a kitchen, a dining area, and three detached duplex cottages and opened the Lazy K Bar as their winter operation. In 1942, the ranch was sold. A succession of new owners followed, including a stressed-out Chicago businessman who died at the ranch six years after his purchase. In 1957, a family named Spaulding bought the ranch. The Spauldings operated it until 1975, when it was purchased by William Scott and Rosemary Blowitz. After their deaths, the ranch came under the ownership of their son, with day-to-day operations handled by the Lazy K Bar's longtime manager, Carol Moore.

The small, intimate ranch, located at an altitude of 2,300 feet, is surrounded by mountains and offers a view of the Santa Cruz Valley. The old lodge building, part of the original homestead, remains in active service as the ranch office. The original beams beneath the raised cathedral ceiling are still there, as are the old cement floors, scored to resemble large blocks of tile. Sofas are grouped into a cozy conversational area around the fireplace in the adjoining main lodge, a friendly gathering room for the entire "ranch family."

The ranch was updated and enlarged by various owners through the years, with the last burnt-adobe guest units added in 1983. Today, it offers 23 spacious guest rooms in a convenient horseshoe layout. All the rooms are comfortably furnished and have private baths and individual air-conditioning and heating controls. The rooms open out to a central desert courtyard garden, where citrus trees, saguaros, and eucalyptus trees share space in the bright sun.

Back at the corral, skilled wranglers will match you up with a suitable mount before guiding you along the desert trails. Along the way, they'll keep you entertained with tales of the Wild West. Horses are a major focus at the ranch, where a quarter-horse breeding program provides an attraction for young and old. The Lazy K Bar is also the first guest ranch to offer "team penning"—working with cattle in an arena—to its guests.

In the evenings, hearty meals are served family-style in the large dining room. The exception is Saturday night, when thick, juicy T-bone steaks are mesquite-grilled over an open rock-pit barbecue and served under the stars. If you are one of those people who feels that a stay at a dude ranch is incomplete without hayrides, square dancing, and country singers, you'll be happy to know that these attractions are scheduled on a regular basis at the Lazy K Bar.

Rates

The 23 rooms with private baths are available for $92.50 to $175, depending on the season. The American plan includes breakfast, lunch, dinner, and horseback riding. The ranch is open year-round. Major credit cards are accepted.

Amenities

The ranch offers a heated pool, an outdoor spa, laundry facilities, a store, a dining room, a television room, a BYOB bar, a library, lighted tennis courts, billiard tables, and facilities for volleyball, basketball, shuffleboard, horseshoes, and ping-pong.

The Lodge on the Desert

The Lodge on the Desert
P.O. Box 42500
306 North Alvernon Way
Tucson, Arizona 85733
phone: 800-456-5634 or 520-435-3366
fax: 520-327-5834
Dirk Oldenburg, manager

WHEN THE LODGE ON THE DESERT opened in 1936, it sat on a lonely dirt road in the desert far from town. But the city stretched eastward as the years passed, swallowing up the open spaces that once surrounded the hacienda-style guest lodge. Today, it sits squarely in the city, with traffic whizzing by on paved streets. But you'd never know, because behind the thick adobe walls high enough to block the city from sight and low enough for a view of the mountains, you'd swear you were out in the sticks.

There's a feeling of both seclusion and spaciousness at this time-honored lodge, where the focus is on the Southwest's love for outdoor living. Eleven flat-roofed adobe-and-stucco casitas with ocotillo-covered verandas and intimate courtyards are set along meandering paths on six acres of landscaped grounds. Sunlight filtering through cactus ribs creates interesting patterns on walls inlaid with Mexican tiles. Flowers spilling from tubs under archways add to the lodge's Old World charm.

Constructed in 1931, the structure that now serves as the lodge's main building was designed by a New York architect who had never set foot in Tucson. The large, four-bedroom Spanish-style house with horse corral, bunkhouse, and fish pond was built as a private residence for a Massachusetts couple named Quinsler. It was sold a few years later to owners who added a guest room and a swimming pool. In 1936, the complex was purchased by Cornelia and Homer Lininger and converted into a guest lodge.

Schuyler W. Lininger, son of the lodge's founders, grew up on the property and eventually bought it from his parents in 1947. He was there on opening day, when the lodge offered seven guest rooms, and he watched as it grew through six decades into the present sprawling complex with 37 guest rooms and numerous public rooms, including an award-winning restaurant. Lininger continued the family tradition as owner/innkeeper until the spring of 1997, when the lodge was sold to Red Rock Resort of Phoenix.

The inn's office, a guest lounge, and a library are housed in the original building, which has old brick floors, a handsome fireplace, and an unobstructed view of the swimming pool and the Santa Catalina Mountains. The sprawling dining room curves around a shady courtyard with a fish pond and a fountain. The colorful Mexican decor features tin chandeliers and a kiva fireplace. The spacious, individually decorated casitas have redtile floors, beam ceilings, and comfortable ranch-style furnishings. The rooms vary in size. Some have fireplaces and sun decks, most have corner windows, and one even has a private indoor pool. All have private baths and televisions hidden inside handsome armoires so as not to intrude.

Although the lodge is open all year, it is known primarily as a winter resort for returning guests fleeing the cold temperatures back home. The convenient in-town location is a draw for those who want to take in Tucson's many attractions, historical and otherwise.

Rates

The 37 rooms are available for $54 to $195, depending on the season; high season is from mid-January to March 31. Continental breakfast is included. Credit cards are accepted. Children are welcome. The lodge is open all year.

Amenities

The rooms have private baths, telephones, and televisions. The lodge offers a swimming pool, a library, a restaurant, off-street parking, and wheelchair access.

Location

The lodge is on Alvernon Way, northeast of Broadway.

Peppertrees Bed-and-Breakfast Inn

724 East University Boulevard
Tucson, Arizona 85719
phone: 800-348-5763 or 520-622-7167
fax: 520-622-5959
Marjorie Martin, innkeeper

THE TWO CALIFORNIA PEPPER TREES which provide the name for this neat red-brick 1905 Victorian structure are nearly as old as the house itself. The trees and house are set back from the road in a raised position designed to take advantage of passing breezes, which must have provided welcome relief for the structure's first inhabitants, the Batterton family.

Peppertrees Bed-and-Breakfast Inn

When tuberculosis-ridden Harry Batterton arrived in Tucson with his family in 1906, he was not expected to live long. But the desert climate provided the magic cure for Batterton, who promptly recovered and went on to enjoy an active family life and a colorful professional life as a cowhand, banker, forest ranger, and politician until his death at age 84.

When the Batterton family purchased the home in 1914, the University of Arizona and its surrounding area were beginning to develop. One-acre lots were selling for $5 to $20. The Old Pueblo Trolley's electric streetcars traveled a three-mile loop from downtown Tucson to the university campus. By 1930, the neighborhood had become respectable enough to provide an easy cover for gangsters who liked to vacation in Tucson. One member of the Batterton family remembers watching the capture of John Dillinger at the house across the street in the 1930s.

The classic one-story home was built with thick walls and high ceilings. It consisted of three rooms, a dirt cellar, a back porch for cooking, and an outhouse. The Battertons expanded and updated the structure as needed during their residency, which ended in 1947. For a time, the structure housed an antique shop and rental quarters for university students. In 1977, it was purchased by Marjorie Martin and her son, Chris. Several years of painting, refinishing, and refurbishing followed, resulting in a handsomely restored structure filled with antiques and period furniture from Marjorie's family home in England. A new bathroom, French doors, and two separate guesthouses were added, and the backyard was transformed into a tranquil garden retreat. Marjorie finally opened Pepper-trees Bed-and-Breakfast Inn in 1988. A few years after opening, the Martins purchased the adjacent 1917 bungalow, renovated it, and added it to the inn, allowing guests a variety of options.

The main house features original 12-foot ceilings, pine floors covered with Oriental rugs, and a romantic guest room with Victorian decor, three walls of windows, and a view of the patio, where tiny lights twinkle in the trees at night. Two attractive and comfortably furnished guest rooms with private baths and a living room are located in the adjacent structure. Behind the garden patio are two Southwestern-style guest duplexes, each with contemporary decor, two upstairs bedrooms, a fully equipped kitchen, a living room, and a private patio.

Breakfast, a gourmet affair definitely worth rising for, is served buffet-style in the main house's dining room. It features items from the innkeeper's cookbook, *Recipes from Peppertrees*. Tucson's pleasant climate and the inn's colorful garden make an irresistible combination, and many guests prefer to carry breakfast outdoors to a table on the sunny patio, near the trickling Mexican-tile fountain.

Rates

The three rooms and the two two-bedroom guesthouses are available for $78 to $150. Breakfast and afternoon tea are included. Smoking is not permitted indoors. No pets are allowed. Personal checks, Visa, and MasterCard are accepted. Check-in is from 2 P.M. to 6 P.M. and check-out at 11 A.M.

Amenities

All the rooms have private baths. The guesthouses have phones, televisions, washers, and dryers. The inn offers off-street parking. It is within easy walking distance of the University of Arizona, shops, cafes, and museums.

Location

The inn is in the West University Historic District on University Boulevard between Euclid and Fourth Avenues.

Tanque Verde Ranch

Tanque Verde Ranch

14301 East Speedway Boulevard
Tucson, Arizona 85748
phone: 800-234-DUDE or 520-296-6275
fax: 520-721-9426
Bob Cote, manager

SITTING ON THE BROAD, low-slung porch at the Tanque Verde Ranch, you can almost see Mexican vaqueros roping reluctant steers and swaying stagecoaches rumbling by on their way to Tucson. You may imagine you've time-traveled back to the Old West at this 125-year-old ranch, which looks like a scene from a cowboy movie.

Tanque Verde is Spanish for "Green Tank," the name given to the land at the base of the Rincon Mountains, where artesian pools once lay beside creek beds. In 1868, Emilio Carrillo, a rancher from Sonora, Mexico, found the area an ideal place to establish his cattle ranch. Apache raids were common in those days, and cavalry patrols from nearby Fort Lowell stopped by to water their horses. Carrillo's cattle ranch prospered. His *R/C* brand was registered in 1904, the same year the rancher was hanged by the neck over a beam in the present-day card room. He survived the hanging but died from complications a few years later.

In the 1920s, the working cattle ranch was converted to a dude ranch by new owner Jim Converse, a wild and brash cattleman. After being convicted of shooting a cowboy at a local bar, Converse sold the operation in 1957 to the Cote family, who began developing the ranch into a world-class Western resort.

Many of the ranch's earliest structures—made from adobe and stone and mesquite and saguaro ribs—are still in use today at this four-star resort, one of the last luxurious outposts of the Old West. One of the oldest buildings is the original ranch house, with its rugged ceiling beams and huge stone fireplace. Although rooms have been added to the structure through the years, the original Territorial architectural style has been retained.

The Tanque Verde Ranch offers the finest in comfort, but the main attraction is the 640 acres of breathtaking natural scenery. Ranch guests can hike, bike, or ride horseback over miles of spectacular mountain trails bordered by giant saguaros. Nature walks, fishing trips, bird banding, tennis, indoor and outdoor swimming, cowboy cookouts, and country-and-western music in the evening are also offered.

The 65 pink-adobe rooms and spacious patio casitas are situated along footpaths and among cactus gardens. The guest rooms have comfortable Western-style furnishings and feature rustic beam ceilings and private baths. Most have beehive fireplaces, tile baths, and sliding doors that open onto private patios and stunning desert and mountain views.

Don't be surprised to hear a language other than your own being spoken here, as the Tanque Verde Ranch ranks high with Europeans wanting to live out their cowboy and cowgirl fantasies.

Rates

The 65 rooms are available on the American plan (which includes three meals a day, horseback riding, and activities) for $195 to $420, depending on the season. High season is mid-December to April 30. No pets are allowed.

Westward Look Resort

245 East Ina Road
Tucson, Arizona 85704
phone: 800-722-2500 or 520-297-1151
fax: 520-297-9023

LONG BEFORE THE FOOTHILLS of the Santa Catalina Mountains over-looking Tucson became studded with luxurious resorts, the structure that houses the Westward Look was there. Tucson's first resort dates to 1912, the year Arizona became the 48th star on the nation's flag.

It was also that year when a Tucson couple, William and Mary Watson, acquired 172 acres far north of town and planned their dream home. They hired Tucson's premier architect, M. J. Starkweather, to design a spacious two-story house with an artist's loft, living quarters, and a Spanish-style patio. Veering from tradition, Starkweather used steel and concrete—disguised to look like adobe—to construct the Watsons' residence, a feature that has ensured the building's excellent state today.

In the 1920s and 1930s, when guest ranches began appearing on the

Arizona landscape, the Watsons built 15 cottages near their residence and invited guests from the East to come and enjoy Tucson's warm winter temperatures. In the early 1940s, the property was sold to Beverly and Bob Nason, who began operating it as a full-fledged guest ranch named Westward Look. The Nasons added 15 more guest rooms.

The resort changed owners in 1972 and 1982 and was expanded at each sale. By 1995, when the Coastal Hotel Group purchased it, the resort boasted 244 suites, three swimming pools, eight tennis courts, a clubhouse, horseback-riding stables, a bar and grill, an award-winning restaurant, and a sports park. The multimillion-dollar renovation launched by the new owners resulted in the incorporation of the original historic home (previously used for administrative offices) into the mainstream of resort activity. The guest rooms were redecorated with a new Southwestern look, a wellness center was built, and the resort became known as an oasis of relaxation, recreation, and rejuvenation.

The Westward Look spreads over 80 acres of landscaped grounds and has received the prestigious AAA Four Diamond Award for 14 consecutive years. Its 244 spacious, air-conditioned rooms are in secluded clusters of two-story buildings surrounded by thick foliage. Each room has a private entrance, a private bath, and a balcony or patio with a view of the mountains or the city. The interiors have white stucco walls and feature

Westward Look Resort

rustic Old World furnishings, carved armoires, and pierced-tin mirrors. The bathrooms have hand-painted ceramic tiles and terra-cotta floors.

One of the most dramatic changes to the resort was the joining of the Vigas Room—the living room of the 1912 residence—to the main lobby. The inviting room has original plank floors, a ceiling made of log beams and vigas (cactus ribs), and wrought-iron chandeliers as big as wagon wheels. Caramel-colored leather sofas flank the fireplace, and old beams protrude through the thick walls above the mantel.

The Westward Look is a self-contained escape where you can play in the sun, be pampered at the spa, and dine on award-winning Southwestern cuisine in the evening. The windows in the dining room and the guest-room balconies offer magnificent views of Tucson twinkling in the distance at night and the purple-tinted Santa Catalina Mountains in the morning.

Rates

The 244 rooms with private baths are available for $109 to $269, depending on the season; call for low summer rates. Check-in is at 4 P.M. and check-out at noon. Credit cards are accepted. Small pets are allowed.

Amenities

Each room has a wet bar and/or a refrigerator, a television, coffee service, a balcony or patio, and an ironing board and iron. The resort offers eight championship tennis courts, a fitness center, a pro shop, a tennis club, horseback riding, three heated pools, three whirlpools, nature and jogging trails, basketball and sand volleyball courts, mountain-bike rentals, a gift shop, a restaurant, a bar and grill with live music, poolside cabanas, room service, and facilities for conventions, meetings, and banquets.

Location

From Interstate 10, exit at Ina Road. The entrance is on Ina Road a half-mile east of Oracle Road.

White Stallion Guest Ranch

White Stallion Guest Ranch

9251 West Twin Peaks Road
Tucson, Arizona 85743
phone: 888-977-2624 or 520-297-0252
fax: 520-744-2786
Cynthia, Russell, and Michael True, owners/managers

THIS RAMBLING 3,000-ACRE RANCH in the desert foothills of the Tucson Mountains continues to operate as a working cattle ranch, the reason for its founding almost a century ago. This may also explain the White Stallion's success as a dude ranch. Guests can't wait to watch real cowboys work the Longhorn cattle herds.

The ranch was founded in the early 1900s, when the structure that now houses the dining room was built of sun-dried adobe to serve as the owner's residence. In the 1930s, ranching operations expanded to include 30,000 pens for chickens and turkeys. Guests began arriving in the early 1940s when Max Zimmerman, a Chicago liquor-store owner, bought the ranch and enlarged the main house, added an office, and had six guest units built by Mexican masons, who crafted the blocks on the ranch. Because Zimmerman had no interest in providing meals for his guests, he had kitchens installed in each unit; these were later removed.

When the property changed hands in 1948, guest operations ceased for a decade. They started again in 1958, when Brew and Marge Towne of Cape Cod, Massachusetts, bought the property. The Townes intended to name the ranch after their favorite horse story, *The Black Stallion*, but found the initials *BS* unacceptable. The name they chose instead is a misnomer, since a white stallion has never been seen on the ranch.

In 1965, the True family from Denver bought the 160-acre ranch. The Trues—including some third-generation family members—continue to operate it today. A forward-thinking family, they began purchasing the surrounding property as Tucson's growth threatened to overtake the open desert around the ranch. Today, the ranch claims nearly five square miles and offers 29 guest rooms and enough horseback-riding activities to challenge the cowboy or cowgirl in all of us.

The guest rooms are in white, flat-roofed Pueblo-style buildings grouped along brick walks bordered by desert. The comfortable, rustic accommodations include eight-foot beam ceilings and Southwestern furnishings with Mexican and Native American accents. All have private baths and brick patios with redwood chairs and chaise lounges, a perfect setting for relaxing and enjoying Arizona's brilliant night skies.

The pens of exotic birds, the petting zoo, and the peacocks that run free around the ranch will delight youngsters. Horseback riders back from a morning trail ride can unwind in the heated pool or the indoor redwood hot tub. The meal bell clangs three times a day, calling guests to the original ranch house, which has been expanded to include a large dining room featuring tables inlaid with colorful tiles and hand-carved chairs from Mexico. The adjacent kitchen is in the original living room, and the entrance hall and gift shop occupy the former courtyard areas. The ranch's setting seems ideal for Western films, so it's not surprising to learn that many scenes for the television series *High Chaparral* were filmed here.

Rates

Rooms are available for $128 to $164 daily and $840 to $1,113 weekly, depending on the season. The rates include all meals and horseback riding. Credit cards are not accepted.
No pets are allowed.
The ranch is closed June, July, August, and September.

Wild Horse Ranch Resort

6801 North Camino Verde
Tucson, Arizona 85743
phone: 520-744-1012
fax: 520-579-3991

YOU ALMOST EXPECT TO SEE John Wayne gallop by at this historic ranch, which rambles over 30 acres of desert at the base of the Tucson Mountains. In fact, the ranch so pleased the Duke that he had a guest room built on the grounds for his exclusive use whenever he was in town filming one of his numerous Westerns. John Wayne wasn't the only celebrity who spent time here, although he appears in most of the old photos on display in the rustic main lodge. Other famous guests have included Jimmy Stewart, Art Linkletter, Virginia Mayo, and the archduke of Austria.

The oldest rock-and-adobe building on the ranch dates to 1890, when the site was a base camp for silver and gold miners. Legend has it that gold was buried on the property long ago. Although many search parties set out to find it, the gold was never discovered.

During the early 1900s, the property, then known as the Eureka Ranch, consisted of several hundred acres of saguaro-studded landscape. Through the years, the original buildings were enlarged. New ones were added after Chicagoan Howard Miller purchased the property in 1930 and opened it as a guest ranch. Short-term owners followed Miller. Eventually, the ranch developed into a rustic Western resort offering horseback riding, a swimming pool, a waterfall, lily ponds, tennis courts, and comfortable ranch-style lodgings.

The guest rooms are in an assortment of simple single-story buildings, including the original adobe casitas built around the turn of the century. They are arranged along gravel paths bordered by cactus gardens. Each casita is equipped with a private bathroom and heating and cooling systems, but appliances have been kept to a minimum. The focus here is on the ranch's natural desert setting and Old West flavor, so you'll find no televisions or telephones in the rooms, though they are available in the main lodge.

For guests who have always wanted to appear in a Western, the ranch offers "The Original Cowboy Movie Fantasy Camp." Participants are outfitted in Western attire and star in a movie that can later be taken home on videocassette.

Rates

The 25 rooms and casitas with private baths are available for $55 to $110; weekly and group rates are available. Continental breakfast is included. Pets are permitted. The ranch is open all year.

Amenities

The ranch offers a well-stocked library, a dining room, a bar, a lobby, horseback riding, hiking, a swimming pool, a wellness center, and tennis, volleyball, and badminton courts.

Willcox

Muleshoe Ranch

Muleshoe Ranch

Rural Route 1, Box 1542
Willcox, Arizona 85643
phone: 520-586-7072

NESTLED FAR OFF THE HIGHWAY in the foothills of the Galiuro Mountains on 49,000 acres of riparian desert, the Muleshoe Ranch is the most peaceful and remote escape in this book. To reach it, you must travel for an hour along a bumpy dirt road that winds for 30 miles. But the trip is well worth the trouble, because this historic ranch contains a treasure some consider more precious than gold: natural hot springs bubbling from a hill. It also has a history that reads like a Western novel.

The Muleshoe story began in 1875, when a former New Yorker, Dr. Glendy King, staked a claim for a 160-acre homestead where a stream of rejuvenating 115-degree water flowed from a hill. Seeking better health in the West, King discovered his cure in the soothing waters of the hot springs, and he dreamed of developing the site into a commercial success. In 1882, he erected two rectangular adobe buildings and a few crude wooden bathhouses. But his hopes were dashed by those who ruled the land: marauding Apache, cattle rustlers, and stage robbers. King died two years later from a gunshot wound received during a property dispute.

The land was then sold to cattle baron Henry Clay Hooker. Expanding on King's dream, Hooker enlarged the existing structures, added a few new ones, and launched a newspaper promoting the healing waters at Hooker's Hot Springs. The response was overwhelming. By 1890, a post office and a store were added. Plans were also made to build a sanitarium. The Hooker era was one of success peppered by seasons of severe drought and fierce flooding.

In 1906, the ranch was sold to a wealthy Philadelphian, Demming Isaacson, who is credited with moving the operation into the 20th century. Isaacson installed generators, built new structures, and planted shade trees and flowers, creating the ranch's present U-shaped layout.

Periods of flooding and drought returned in the early 1920s, resulting in the foreclosure of Isaacson's mortgage in 1927. The next owner was a well-heeled Cleveland divorcee, Jessica McMurray. In the 1930s, McMurray built a small stone cottage for her sister, enlarged the dining wing, and furnished the rooms with elegant Oriental rugs and antiques. During the McMurray years, the Muleshoe operated as a private guest ranch of sorts. The spacious Spanish-style home that today houses the headquarters of the Arizona chapter of the Nature Conservancy was built by a guest during Jessica's absence, causing a promptly severed friendship upon the unhappy owner's return.

After Jessica's death in 1950, the property was sold again. More owners came and went. In 1972, a lightning storm destroyed sections of the ranch's central and southern wings. A decade later, the property was sold to the Nature Conservancy, which continues to jointly own and operate the Muleshoe and its preserve of streams, springs, canyons, and desert with the United States Forest Service and the Bureau of Land Management.

The guest rooms at the ranch are a mixture of original and renovated historic buildings. Four restored casitas face a grassy central patio, and a rustic two-room stone cabin is located 100 yards away. The accommodations, which vary in size from a one-room studio to the four-room King Casita, have well-equipped kitchens, private baths, and attractive furnishings. Two rooms have wood-burning stoves. The building burned by lightning was renovated in 1992 and houses a lounge, where guests can look through an interesting collection of old photographs.

Overnight guests are encouraged to experience the soothing waters of the hot springs in soaking tubs. Hikers, photographers, and birders can explore the area's many hiking trails and attend the natural-history programs offered periodically through the Nature Conservancy.

Rates

The five cabins are available for $70 to $100 (double occupancy). No food services are offered. MasterCard, Visa, and American Express are accepted. No pets are allowed. Overnight guests are not accepted in June, July, and August.

Amenities

The cabins have kitchens and baths; some have wood-burning stoves. The ranch offers common gathering rooms, hot springs, a gift shop, and camping facilities.

Location

The ranch is 30 miles northwest of Willcox. Follow Airport Road north over Interstate 10 as it becomes a dirt road. Continue 15 miles to a fork. Veer right and go another 15 miles. Drive under the Muleshoe Ranch sign and continue 0.75 mile. Turn left at the entrance and cross Hot Springs Wash to reach the ranch's headquarters.

Triangle T Guest Ranch

Triangle T Guest Ranch

**P.O. Box 218
Dragoon, Arizona 85609
phone: 520-586-7533
L. Jayne Drotning, manager**

THIS REMOTE, RUSTIC GUEST RANCH occupies 160 acres of gently sloping land at the foothills of the Dragoon Mountains in Texas Canyon, an area in southeastern Arizona where giant boulders are piled high in dramatic formations.

Established in 1922, the Triangle T is one of the oldest guest ranches in the state and claims an interesting history. In 1929, it was awarded to Catherine Tutt after the breach of a contract-to-marry suit. The ranch has welcomed many dignitaries, including John F. Kennedy, General John Pershing, and members of the Rockefeller and Vanderbilt families. During World War II, it was the center of intrigue when a group of Japanese spies was ordered to the ranch by President Franklin Roosevelt. For a time, Dr. Leon Silver, former director of NASA, had his Cal Tech geology students complete their theses here during the summers. In 1975, "The Last Cattle Drive," a bicentennial salute to the American cowboy, originated at the ranch. The drive ended in Tucson 30 days and 350 miles later.

The accommodations are less than luxurious at the ranch, where restoration is an ongoing process. Guests stay in one- and two-room ranch-style cottages and in a comfortable bunkhouse. Some rooms have rugged stone fireplaces and refrigerators, and some are in duplex buildings with wide flagstone porches stretching across the entire front. The furnishings—including four-poster beds, braided rugs, and claw-foot tubs in some rooms—reflect the laid-back ranch lifestyle. The two-room suites feature sitting areas with sofa beds and roomy baths.

Meals are served in the old adobe main lodge or sometimes under the stars around a campfire. A spacious rustic saloon is located beside a fenced pool area. At the corral, horses stand ready for a ride along one of the ranch's many trails.

RV owners and campers can also enjoy an escape at this remote ranch, which provides full hookups and showers, along with pool, restaurant, and horse privileges.

Rates

Accommodations for up to 30 guests are available in one-room and two-room cottages for $50 to $65 and in a dormitory-style bunkhouse for $40. Cottage rates are based on double occupancy. The charge for each additional guest is $15; there is no charge for children under six years of age. Campsites with full RV hookups are available for $14, sites with no hookups for $8, and tent campsites for $4. Pets are allowed in the camping area only.

Amenities

The ranch offers a pool, a saloon, a restaurant, horseback riding, and hiking trails.

Tombstone

Buford House

Buford House

113 East Safford Street
Tombstone, Arizona 85638
phone: 800-263-6762 or 520-457-3969
Brenda Reger, owner/hostess

TOMBSTONE, "THE TOWN TOO TOUGH TO DIE," is mighty proud of its Old West history. Costumed gunslingers, gamblers, and dance-hall girls strut their stuff and mingle with the crowds of tourists on the streets, which look like a scene right out of a Hollywood Western. Nearby at the OK Corral, noisy shootouts are staged regularly to reenact the famous gunfight between the Earps and the Clantons. This event was surely the topic of many conversations at the Buford House, located a few blocks away.

The Territorial-style adobe home with the wide wraparound porch has been home to many of Tombstone's most prominent citizens. Built in 1880 for wealthy mine owner George Buford, the two-story structure was also the residence of Arizona's last stagecoach driver, two sheriffs, a mayor, a marshal, and a state senator. Today, it belongs to Brenda Reger, a former White House consultant who spent many years commuting between the nation's capital and tiny Tombstone before opening her historic bed-and-breakfast in 1990. An interesting collection of photos taken during Reger's White House days is on display in the foyer.

As you would expect in a structure listed on the National Register of Historic Places, the interior features many antiques and other handsome period pieces. Arrowhead inlays add interest to the rugged rock fireplace in the parlor. In the corner stands an authentic fortune-teller box dating to the 1920s. It still dispenses fortunes when fed a coin.

Guest rooms are on both levels of the home. The largest, the Garden Room, is downstairs off the main entry hall. It features a private entrance, a private bath, an original sunken concrete bathtub, and a fireplace. The three upstairs rooms—the Victorian Room, the Nellie Cashman Room, and the Buford Room—all share a bath, but each room has a sink and mirror for a quick freshening up. At the end of the upstairs hall is a headless dressmaker's form clothed in a maternity dress from the 1880s, an item said to startle sleepwalkers.

Breakfast, a sit-down affair served in the downstairs dining room at 8 A.M., 9 A.M., or 10 A.M., features fresh items from Reger's garden. Guests often take their final cup of coffee out to the porch that wraps around the front and side of the house, where they can watch goldfish in the pond and birds at the feeders.

Rates

The five guest rooms are available for $65 to $95. Full breakfast is included. Children under age four and pets are not allowed. Credit cards are not accepted. No smoking is permitted indoors.

Amenities

Two of the guest rooms have private baths. The remaining three rooms share a bath. Sinks are in each room. The inn offers a large porch.

Location

The inn is near the intersection of Safford and Second Streets, one block south of AZ 80 (Fremont Street).

Priscilla's Bed-and-Breakfast

P.O. Box 700
101 North Third Street
Tombstone, Arizona 85638
phone: 520-457-3844
Barbara and Larry Gray, owners/innkeepers

THIS CREAM-COLORED VICTORIAN with a pillared front porch and its original picket fence sits on a quiet corner two blocks from the OK Corral and downtown Tombstone. Built in 1904 by an affluent attorney, it is listed on the National Register of Historic Places and is the only remaining two-story clapboard country Victorian house in Tombstone.

In 1990, it was purchased by Barbara and Larry Gray. They spent two years restoring the house: adding a new stairway, refinishing the original floors, and sprucing up the original wainscoting, the built-in cupboards, the pocket doors, and the gaslight fixtures. They painted with authentic Victorian colors and decorated the home in a romantic country Victorian

Priscilla's Bed-and-Breakfast

style with antique furnishings and white lace curtains. When they were finally finished in 1992, they named the charming house after Barbara's mother and opened it as a bed-and-breakfast.

A handsome staircase leads to three guest rooms: the Primrose Room, the Violet Room, and the Rose Room. They share the floor with a bathroom that includes a spacious tiled shower. All the bedrooms have double beds, sinks, and vanities and are decorated with floral prints and antique furnishings.

Breakfast is served downstairs at a round oak dining table covered in lace. Barbara's home-style morning meals include her hot-from-the-oven breads and homemade jams and jellies. A wicker chair on the front porch is a good place to sip a last cup of coffee or tea and admire the tiered fountain and the winding paths and gardens which surround the house. The brick walk leading from the porch to the street was created from a former chimney. Across the street is St. Paul's Episcopal Church, built in 1876 and considered Arizona's first Protestant church.

Tombstone Boarding House
Bed-and-Breakfast Inn

P.O. Box 906
108 North Fourth Street
Tombstone, Arizona 85638
phone: 520-457-3716
fax: 520-457-3038
Shirley Villarin, innkeeper

TOMBSTONE'S IMAGE as a rip-roaring, gunslinging Old West town is kept alive with regularly scheduled shootouts and brawls downtown on Allen Street. Tourists flock to watch the action at the Bird Cage Theater, Big Nose Kate's Saloon, and the Crystal Palace, and there's usually a crowd at the OK Corral watching the reenactment of the famous gunfight. A few blocks away at the Tombstone Boarding House, however, all is quiet and refined.

This charming bed-and-breakfast consists of two white adobe houses with tin roofs sitting side by side behind a prim white picket fence. The

Tombstone Boarding House Bed-and-Breakfast Inn

structures were built in the early 1880s, when Tombstone was at its wild-est. The first house, the residence of Tombstone's first bank manager, was remodeled and enlarged in the 1930s. The second house is the former Barrows Boarding House, where, according to legend, notorious gun-slinger Buckskin Frank Leslie roomed in the 1880s. The story goes that the inebriated Leslie, wanting to prove to his wife that he could shoot drunk or sober, shot her silhouette into the wall of his room. The wall was later plastered over. Another legend has it that Billy Clanton, shot during the 1881 OK Corral gunfight, may have died at the boarding-house. This may be the reason his ghost is said to appear occasionally. In the 1930s, artist H. E. Wenck built a studio onto the structure; its pic-ture window allows a spectacular view of the surrounding mountains.

Current owners Shirley and Ted Villarin purchased the two structures in 1988 and converted them into Tombstone's first bed-and-breakfast. The Villarins live in one building, and the inn's guests are housed in seven rooms in the old boardinghouse and an eighth room in what was once a miner's cabin. Each guest room has a private entrance, a private bath, and gleaming fir, maple, or oak floors. Cast-iron beds, hand-carved head-boards, claw-foot tubs, and other interesting antique furnishings gath-ered from around Cochise County re-create the ambiance of the 1880s. An antique army cot from nearby Fort Huachuca is a big hit with children.

Guests gather at the Villarins' house to watch television in the living room and enjoy Shirley's hearty homemade breakfasts, prepared and served in the adjoining blue-and-white kitchen.

Rates

The eight rooms (five with double beds, two with queens, and one with a king) are available for $65 to $80. Full breakfast and evening wine are included. Check-in is from 3 P.M. to 6 P.M. and check-out at 11 A.M. Credit cards are not accepted. No smoking is allowed indoors.

Amenities

The rooms have private baths and private entrances. A television and a piano are in the living room. The inn is within walking distance of downtown attractions.

Location

The inn is on North Fourth Street two blocks north of AZ 80 (Fremont Street). It is on the right just beyond the Safford Street intersection.

Victoria's Bed-and-Breakfast

P.O. Box 37
211 East Toughnut Street
Tombstone, Arizona 85638
phone: 520-457-3677
Victoria Collins, owner/innkeeper

THIS SMALL WHITE ADOBE INN, trimmed in bright red and roofed with tin, sits next door to the historic 1882 Cochise County Courthouse. The old courthouse is a museum today, but back in the late 1800s, it provided a customer base for Emily Morton's boardinghouse and house of pleasure. It's said that Morton suffered a violent death in the house,

Victoria's Bed-and-Breakfast

which may be the reason her disgruntled spirit returns every now and then to set the chandeliers swinging.

The modest one-story structure was built in 1880, when Tombstone was enjoying its heyday as a prosperous silver-mining town. Traces of the house's elegance remain today, including original rose-etched leaded-glass windows and hardwood ceilings and floors. After the courthouse closed in 1929, the house adapted to a variety of roles. At different times, it housed offices, a gaming house, rental quarters, shops, and a private residence. In 1946, an addition was built onto the back of the house.

In the mid-1990s, the neglected home was sold to Victoria Collins. Bolstered by her affinity for the Victorian era, she painted and refurbished the place, cleverly creating a bed-and-breakfast, which opened in 1996.

The quaint cottage sits behind a white wrought-iron fence in the shade of a sprawling mulberry tree. As you'd expect, the decor is lace-curtained Victorian. The inn's three attractive guests room have wooden floors, private baths, queen-size beds, and cable television. During summer and fall, continental breakfast is served in the spacious dining room; during winter, spring, and special events, a full and hearty breakfast is served.

From the ramada in the backyard, guests can view the surrounding mountains. They can also see the gallows next door, which peeks above the courthouse walls.

Rates

The three rooms are available for $55 to $75, depending on the season. Breakfast is included. Visa and MasterCard are accepted. No children or pets are allowed. Check-in is at 4 P.M. and check-out at 11 A.M.

Amenities

The rooms have private baths, cable television, and queen-size beds. The inn offers a Jacuzzi, a smokers' room, a porch, and a backyard patio and ramada. It is within walking distance of downtown attractions.

Location

The inn is on Toughnut Street near the corner of Third Street.

Amado

Rex Ranch

P.O. Box 636
Amado, Arizona 85645
phone: 888-REXRANCH or 520-398-2914
fax: 520-398-8229
e-mail: rexranch@theriver.com

LIKE MANY GUEST RANCHES in southern Arizona, the Rex Ranch has a history dating back to the 1800s, when it was part of a Spanish land grant. When the Gadsden Purchase of 1853 repositioned the Arizona-Mexico border, land which once belonged to Mexico became Arizona territory. The first American to own the 4,000-acre spread known as the

Montosa Ranch was W. Knibbie, a government trapper and cattleman who operated it as a cattle ranch.

In the 1930s, Knibbie sold the property to a Texan named Rex Hamaker, who remodeled and enlarged the facilities and began operating a dude ranch. Twenty years later, a couple named Donnau purchased the property and combined the dude-ranch operation with a cattle ranch. In the mid-1980s, a portion of the ranch was sold to a couple named Blake, who launched an ambitious restoration project which included the updating of all 14 buildings, the addition of a conference center, and extensive landscaping. When the Nygaard family, the current owners, acquired the ranch in 1995, it added a restaurant and a health spa.

The ranch, which sits on 50 acres of high chaparral desert, is reached by following a mile-long dirt road to the entrance, an experience sure to charm the boots right off you. Portions of the thick adobe walls that have withstood the wind, rain, and sun for more than 170 years form the nucleus of this interesting guest ranch. Painted a striking coral pink and

Rex Ranch

trimmed in bright blue, the ranch resembles an Old World hacienda. An old bell hangs in an alcove high above the rustic wooden entry gates. Open the gates and you're in a colorful enclosed courtyard. In one corner, a cozy sitting area is arranged around a fireplace; across the patio, water splashes in a tiered fountain; and nearby, a handful of tables is set for dining. The excellent restaurant is located in the original ranch house. Guests dine on Nouveau Southwestern dishes that combine the area's native flavors with those of Europe.

To the right of the courtyard is an inviting living room with giant log ceiling beams, a fireplace with a raised hearth, and comfortable leather sofas; guests gather here to mingle, read, and play the piano. Twenty-two spacious guest rooms and casitas, all with private baths, are located behind the enclosed courtyard. The rustic Southwestern decor includes hand-painted furniture, adobe walls, and Native American artwork. Paved walks bordered by desert gardens lead to serene sanctuaries, flowing fountains, and a swimming pool. And everywhere, the smell of roses drifts over from the ranch's bountiful rose garden.

Rates

The rooms are available for $105 to $135, depending on the season. The casitas (suites) rent for $225. Weekly, monthly, group, AARP, and AAA rates are available. Breakfast is included. Special spa packages are offered. Credit cards are accepted.

Amenities

The ranch offers a pool, a health spa, massages, manicures, pedicures, equestrian services, a conference facility, a restaurant, gardens, and gathering areas.

Location

The ranch is 37 miles south of Tucson off Interstate 19. Take Exit 48 to Amado Road. Turn east and drive a mile to the ranch; watch for the signs.

Tubac / Tumacacori

Valle Verde Ranch Bed-and-Breakfast

Valle Verde Ranch Bed-and-Breakfast

P.O. Box 157
Tumacacori, Arizona 85640
phone/fax: 520-398-2246
Alexandra and Giorgio, owners/innkeepers

NESTLED UNDER TOWERING TREES and surrounded by flowering shrubs, this charming Mission-style hacienda was built in 1936. Constructed of adobe with a concrete basement, the spacious 4,800-square-foot structure was once the headquarters of a 1,900-acre cattle ranch and quarter-horse operation. Several owners later, in 1995, the sprawling home opened as a bed-and-breakfast offering three guest rooms and two separate casitas located on six acres beside the banks of the Santa Cruz River.

An arched entry opens to an interior with terra-cotta floors, rustic fireplaces, hand-hewn mesquite beams, and vaulted ceilings. Oversized windows and glass-paneled doors create a light-filled interior, which is furnished throughout with European antiques. At the rear, an airy wrap-around room opens to a terraced courtyard with an outdoor spa and clay pots brimming with colorful blooms. Breakfast is a leisurely sit-down affair with linens and silver, served on the round table in the dining room.

The three guest rooms in the main house have private baths, televisions, and elegant antique furnishings. The smallest, a former maid's room, has a double sleigh bed, a private entrance, and a patio. A few steps from the main house are two separate guest units with kitchenettes and ramadas; one has a Jacuzzi.

The inn is in one of the most historically significant areas in Arizona, where Spanish missionary Eusebio Kino visited the Pima Indian village of Tumacacori in 1691. Construction began on a massive adobe church around 1800, but marauding Apache, a lack of funds, and harsh winters prevented its completion. Declared a National Monument in 1908, the mission is located approximately four miles from the inn. Another nearby historic site is the quaint village of Tubac, established by the Spanish in 1752. Tubac was the first European settlement in what is now Arizona and the site of the state's first newspaper. Today, it is a colorful artists' colony. Its motto—"Where art and history meet"—is promoted by a growing number of studios and galleries displaying arts and crafts by local artists.

Rates

The three rooms and two separate units are available for $80 to $135; rates are adjusted for longer stays. Breakfast is included for guests staying in the main house. Credit cards are not accepted. Smoking is not permitted. No pets are allowed. Check-in is from 3 P.M. to 6 P.M. and check-out at 11 A.M.

Amenities

The rooms have private baths and televisions; some have VCRs. The separate units have kitchenettes. The ranch offers comfortable common rooms, a sunroom, and a courtyard with an outdoor spa.

Location

The ranch is south of Tucson off Interstate 19. Take Exit 34 and drive under the interstate to East Frontage Road. The ranch is located a quarter-mile south of Tubac.

Sonoita

The Vineyard Bed-and-Breakfast

The Vineyard Bed-and-Breakfast

P.O. Box 1227
92 South Los Encinos Road
Sonoita, Arizona 85637
phone: 520-455-4749
Ron and Sue DeCosmo, owners/innkeepers

AGED OAK TREES AND ACRES OF VINEYARDS surround this adobe hacienda, which sits on a hilltop at an elevation of 5,100 feet and offers stunning views of grasslands and mountain vistas. This is southern Arizona's high country, known for its Longhorn cattle ranches and Arabian horse farms. It is also the area that provides the grapes for Arizona's growing wine industry.

The Spanish-style structure which houses the Vineyard Bed-and-Breakfast was originally called the Hacienda Los Encinos, built in 1916 as the main house of a large horse ranch. During the early 1930s, when dude ranches were sprouting up around the state, the hacienda and its grounds served for a time as a guest ranch. After a succession of owners, a 20-acre parcel of the ranch including the house was purchased in 1994 by Ron and Sue DeCosmo, who created an inviting bed-and-breakfast.

Before the DeCosmos opened their inn to guests in 1995, there was much work to be done in the neglected house. Wiring and plumbing had to be brought up to code. A new commercial range with a convection oven and an infrared broiler was installed in the kitchen under the copper hood which has been in the house for as long as anyone can remember. The old archways and Mexican-tile floors are there, too. They blend well with the owners' interesting antiques, which appear throughout the house.

Three guest rooms with private baths and private entrances are located at one end of the main house. A few steps away, guests can chase away the evening chill in front of the huge stone fireplace in the living room or the old beehive fireplace in the kitchen. Behind the main house is the inn's most private accommodation, a charming Southwestern-style casita with a cozy sitting room and a private bath.

Breakfast is served in the main house at tables in the bright eastward-facing sunroom. The menu often includes fresh eggs from the inn's resident hens and home-baked breads and scones prepared with apples, peaches, and almonds grown on the property. A walled patio with a large pool is on the side of the house. It offers a good view of the inn's namesake, the vineyards, which are scheduled for replanting after years of neglect.

Patagonia

Circle Z Ranch

**P.O. Box 194
Patagonia, Arizona 85624
phone: 520-394-2525
Betsy and Bryan Laselle, managers**

THE CIRCLE Z RANCH is everything a historic guest ranch should be: it is rich in history, landscape, horses, and hospitality. The Circle Z dates back to 1925, the golden age of dude ranching, when a family named Zinsmeister purchased the 5,000-acre spread—located in a remote valley at the base of the Santa Rita Mountains—from the homesteading family that had staked its claim to the land in 1874.

Circle Z Ranch

The Circle Z, which is the oldest continuously operating dude ranch in the state, was the brainchild of the Zinsmeisters. After building an adobe Spanish-style main residence and separate cottages to accommodate 24 guests, they opened the Circle Z in 1926. More adobe cottages were added a few years later, increasing the guest capacity to 70.

The ranch was designed as a winter escape. The average stay was one month, but some well-heeled families remained the entire season, arriving in private railway cars which sat at the Patagonia station through their entire stay. Along with first-class accommodations and dining, the Circle Z offered guests a polo field, miles of riding trails, and fine horses bred, raised, and trained on the ranch.

During World War II, the travel business began to wither, and the ranch changed hands several times. In 1949, Chicagoan Fred Fendig purchased the Circle Z. He operated it for the next 25 years. During the Fendig era, the Circle Z was discovered by Hollywood film crews, who made such Westerns as *Broken Lance* (starring Spencer Tracy) and *Monte Walsh* (with Lee Marvin) on the ranch. When Fendig decided to retire and sell the ranch in 1975, rumors were that it was to be purchased by a corporation and developed. The speculation ended when Mr. and Mrs. Preston Nash of Ohio purchased the ranch and promised to preserve the traditions Mrs. Nash remembered from her visits as a child, when the Zinsmeisters owned the Circle Z.

Today, buff-colored adobe guests cottages trimmed in turquoise are scattered about the scenic plateau on which the ranch lies. The Casa Rosa—a one-story horseshoe-shaped structure draped in sweet-smelling jasmine—has eight guest rooms which open out to a central courtyard. The rooms are decorated in a comfortable, unpretentious Southwestern style and feature original furnishings and hand-painted items from Mexico.

Although the rooms are inviting, the real attraction here is the ranch's 5,000-acre setting. Horseback riding is the number-one activity. The ranch's endless variety of trails allows riders (and hikers and birders) to explore rock canyons, mountains, rolling rangeland, and the banks of the tree-lined Sonoita Creek.

Chowtime at the Circle Z can be a breakfast ride, an outdoor cookout, or a family-style meal in the dining room or on the patio of the main guest lodge. The former Zinsmeister family residence, the lodge is where guests gather to enjoy the warmth of the fire in the rugged fireplace built long ago of native stone.

Rates

The ranch offers accommodations for 45 persons. Weekly rates for single / double rooms with private baths run $749 to $945 per person, depending on the season. Ask about special long-weekend rates. All meals, riding, and use of the ranch facilities are included. The ranch is open from November 1 to May 15. Children are welcome, but pets are not permitted. Credit cards are not accepted.

Amenities

The ranch offers horseback riding, a heated swimming pool, game rooms, hiking trails, and an all-weather tennis court.

Location

The ranch is off AZ 82 about 65 miles southeast of Tucson, four miles southwest of Patagonia, and 15 miles northeast of Nogales.

The Duquesne House Bed-and-Breakfast

The Duquesne House Bed-and-Breakfast

357 Duquesne Street
Patagonia, Arizona 85624
phone: 520-394-2732
Regina Medley, owner/hostess

PATAGONIA'S ORIGINS can be traced to the Gadsden Purchase of 1853, when the rich, fertile land between the Patagonia Mountains and the Santa Rita Mountains was ceded to the United States by Mexico. Soon afterward, homesteading Easterners began arriving in the area, eager to set up cattle ranches on the verdant grasslands, once vast Spanish land grants. When miners discovered the rich supply of silver and lead in the Patagonia Mountains, a mining boom was set off. The railroad soon followed, and before long, Patagonia was a busy shipping center for ore and cattle.

Founded in 1898, the town was originally called Rollin, in honor of wealthy rancher and mine holder Rollin Richardson. The citizens apparently had other ideas, and a year later, the name was changed to Patagonia, which is Spanish for "big foot." Mining operations came to a close in 1959. A few years later, the railroad shut down. The railroad's right of way was dedicated as a park, and the train depot, built in 1900, became the town hall.

By the 1970s, Patagonia had become the quiet, sleepy hamlet it is today, a place offering world-weary visitors—like the birders and naturalists who frequent the Nature Conservancy's Patagonia–Sonoita Creek Preserve—a chance to kick back and watch the birds go by. The town's setting at the base of the mountains has also attracted artists like Regina Medley, whose delightful works decorate her bed-and-breakfast.

The Duquesne House, a long, gray adobe building topped with a peaked tin roof, was constructed in 1905, when the Patagonia Mountains were still producing vast quantities of silver and lead. It was built and named for the owner of the Duquesne Mine. A row of attached apartments served his mining crew. In time, indoor plumbing was added.

By the early 1970s, when Medley, a fiber artist and teacher, arrived from Virginia, the structure was in a sorry state. Recognizing a gem in need of polishing, she purchased the building and began the arduous task of restoration one room at a time. The wood floors were replaced with burnt adobe bricks, the 17-inch-thick walls were repaired, and the former miners' quarters were transformed into three delightful two-room suites with private baths. Buttresses and Santa Fe–style benches were added to the exterior.

Today, the owner's artistic talents shine throughout the rustic inn. The attractive suites have private street entrances, high ceilings, and whimsical wall treatments. They are ideal for travelers who enjoy a bed-and-breakfast atmosphere but feel uneasy about staying in someone else's home.

Rates

The three two-room suites with private baths are available for $70. Full breakfast is included. Credit cards are not accepted. Pets are not permitted. No smoking is allowed.

Amenities

The suites have ceiling fans, radios, sitting rooms, queen-size beds, private entrances, and a shared screened porch. Two of the suites have wood-burning stoves.

Sasabe

Rancho de la Osa

Rancho de la Osa

P.O. Box 1
Sasabe, Arizona 85633
phone: 800-872-6240 or 520-823-4257
fax: 520-823-4238
Richard and Veronica Shultz, owners/innkeepers

TO REALLY GET AWAY from it all, head south to the Rancho de la Osa, a 200-year-old hacienda in a valley between the Sierrita Mountains and Baboquivari, a 7,700-foot peak the Papago Indians believed to be sacred. Considered one of the last great haciendas in North America, it was part of a 3-million-acre land grant which stretched for 200 miles from Altar, Mexico, to Florence, Arizona, a gift from the king of Spain to the Ortiz brothers in 1812.

In 1853, the Gadsden Purchase ceded the ranch to the United States, resulting in its location along the Arizona-Mexico border. The next owner, William Sturgus Spencer, a former member of the Republican National Committee, purchased the property in 1889 and began building an elegant adobe hacienda in a quadrangle design. He spared no expense, importing wood for the floors and stained-glass windows from Europe and transporting the goods from Tucson, some 80 miles away. He added servants' quarters and filled his gardens with a variety of exotic plants.

In 1923, the ranch was sold to a Kansas City couple named Hardgraves, who installed bathtubs, showers, electric lighting, and refrigeration. They made the bumpy road to the ranch passable for automobiles and opened a dude ranch. In 1933, the ranch was leased to Dick Jenkins, who eventually bought it. The ranch attracted dignitaries and celebrities seeking seclusion and relaxation, like Justice William O. Douglas, novelist Margaret Mitchell, and Adlai Stevenson, the governor of Illinois and the Democratic candidate for president in 1952. After his defeat by President Dwight Eisenhower, Stevenson fled to the Rancho de la Osa for rest and privacy, only to have his whereabouts revealed in newspapers across the country.

After Jenkins's death in 1956, the property changed hands a few times and ceased operating as a dude ranch. In 1982, the 640 acres were purchased by the William Davis family, who began a remodeling project to return the ranch to its former status. After the Davises' deaths, the property fell into the hands of current owners Richard and Veronica Schultz, who continue to operate the Rancho de la Osa (*osa* is Spanish for she-bear) according to its rich tradition of hospitality and privacy.

The oldest structure on the grounds is a 250-year-old adobe mission, which has been converted into a cantina. The old mission bell hanging nearby announces mealtimes. Gourmet meals are served outdoors around a huge fireplace made of river stone or inside the century-old hacienda in one of the inviting dining rooms.

Guest rooms and suites are arranged in a square facing a large central courtyard shaded by giant eucalyptus trees. They have thick adobe walls, private baths, wood-burning fireplaces, and tasteful furnishings. A short stroll takes you to the heated pool, the spa, and the corrals. Hawks soar overhead, and in the distance, you can hear horses quickening their pace for an uphill climb. At night, under the stars, owls hoot from the trees in the courtyard and coyotes howl in the dark.

Rates

Rooms and suites are available on the American plan for $130 to $200 daily and $910 to $1,400 weekly per person; if horseback riding is included, the rates are $160 to $225 daily and $1,120 to $1,575 weekly. A minimum stay of two nights is required. Credit cards are accepted. Pets are not allowed. Check-in is at 3 P.M. and check-out at 11 A.M.

Amenities

The rooms have private baths and wood-burning fireplaces. The ranch offers a heated pool, a spa, horseback riding, hiking trails, a cantina, a gift shop, gathering areas, patios, and gardens. Private horseback-riding lessons are available; children must be at least 48 inches tall to ride. Buenos Aires National Wildlife Refuge is only five minutes from the ranch.

Location

The ranch is 66 miles southwest of Tucson. Follow AZ 86/286 south to Sasabe. Watch for the sign announcing the Rancho de la Osa. The ranch is located off the highway on the right. Follow the road into the compound.

San Pedro River Inn

8326 South Hereford Road
Hereford, Arizona 85615
phone: 520-366-5532
Walt and May Kolbe, innkeepers

THE SAN PEDRO RIVER INN sits on 20 acres of ecologically significant land near one of the premier wildlife habitats in the United States.
"Ecotourists" flock to the area hoping to glimpse and perhaps photograph
some of the 300 species of birds and 80 species of amphibians and rep-
tiles that inhabit the San Pedro Riparian National Conservation Area.
Operated by the Bureau of Land Management, this 57,000-acre area ranges
from one to three miles wide and stretches for 36 miles along the San
Pedro River in southeastern Arizona. It attracts birders, hikers, and horseback riders. Many seek accommodations at the San Pedro River Inn, a
five-minute walk from the conservation area.

The structures that house the inn date back to the early 1920s and the
Hereford Dairy Farm, owned by a farmer named McDowell. The original
buildings on the site were the farmer's residence and a bunkhouse for
dairy hands. Through the years, these structures were enlarged and mod-
ernized, and extra buildings were added as the demand for dairy workers
grew. The dairy closed in the 1950s, and the property became a private
hobby farm and corporate getaway. In 1995, the property was sold and
converted into a bed-and-breakfast.

Owner Walt Kolbe grew up on a ranch not far from the inn he now
operates with his wife, May. He remembers a day in 1947 when he accompanied his father to the Hereford Dairy Farm to buy a heifer. It
was his only visit until he returned with May 48 years later. The Kolbes
have cleverly created a country inn offering individual and/or shared accommodations in four separate houses. Named Swallow's Nest, Owl's

Roost, Wren's Haven, and Gray Hawk, the houses have one, two, or three bedrooms, a living room, a kitchen, a bath, heating and cooling systems, and a television; two have fireplaces. Gray Hawk, a two-bedroom block-and-adobe house, is the former dairy bunkhouse and the largest of the guesthouses. With a spacious living and dining room, two bedrooms, and a large kitchen, it doubles as a conference center and a gathering place for inn guests.

The guesthouses are scattered about the property, which features giant cottonwood and pecan trees, picnic areas, an old milk barn, and two ponds which host a variety of wildlife. Complimentary continental breakfasts featuring freshly brewed coffee, juice, and scrumptious breads are provided in the guest quarters. Many prefer to breakfast outside on the porch so they can listen to the birds and enjoy the stunning mountain views.

Rates

The accommodations range from $65 for one room to $200 for an entire house for up to six guests. Continental breakfast is included. Smoking is permitted outdoors only. Supervised children are welcome in the houses. Pets are not allowed in the houses, but runs are available. Traveler's checks, personal checks, and cash are accepted.

Amenities

Each house has a bath, a living room, a kitchen, a television, and heating and cooling systems; some have a fireplace. The inn offers a common gathering room with a VCR, picnic areas, a badminton and horseshoes area, individual corrals and pastures for use by horse owners, five RV spaces with hookups, and laundry facilities.

Location

The inn is on Hereford Road 10.5 miles north of the intersection of AZ 92 and Hereford Road and 18 miles southeast of the junction of AZ 90 and AZ 92.

Bisbee Grand Hotel

Bisbee Grand Hotel

P.O. Box 825
61 Main Street
Old Bisbee, Arizona 85603
phone: 800-421-1909 or 520-432-5900
Bill Thomas, owner

THE PICTURESQUE TOWN OF BISBEE, which clings to the slopes of the Mule Mountains, was nothing more than a copper-mining camp in 1880. But a dozen years later, when the Phelps Dodge Corporation put in a railroad, a real town began to rise in Mule Pass Gulch. By 1908, Bisbee had blossomed into Arizona's largest and most cosmopolitan town, boasting a population of 25,000 and a reputation as "the liveliest spot between El Paso and San Francisco."

During the town's heyday, Bisbee residents enjoyed a sophisticated cultural scene and a roaring night life. They constructed stately brick residences on solid rock foundations, most of which continue to give Bisbee an Old World charm that attracts scores of visitors to its sloping streets.

Those structures that didn't survive were destroyed by the catastrophic fires that swept through the town, a common problem in Arizona at the turn of the century.

The Bisbee Grand Hotel, built in the heart of town in 1906 to house traveling mining executives, burned down two years later and had to be rebuilt. In 1986, the two-story hotel was renovated and restored in the extravagant Victorian style of the Old West. Although it closed a year later, the historic gem caught the eye of current owner Bill Thomas. A former banker and tennis coach, Thomas was in Bisbee for a two-day visit when he became smitten with the lavish landmark. He purchased it and reopened it as a bed-and-breakfast in 1989. Business has been booming ever since.

The Bisbee Grand Hotel is indeed properly named. The romantic Victorian elegance begins as you climb the broad, red-carpeted staircase to the inn, located on the second floor. The old hotel features high ceilings, ornate chandeliers, and a cozy balcony overlooking Main Street. Each of the eight guest rooms has its own distinctive decor. The three spacious suites have private baths, claw-foot tubs, and sitting rooms.

A stay at this romantic inn offers a glamorous return to another era—especially if your room is the ornate Oriental Suite, which features black Cantonese wallpaper and an antique, carved Chinese wedding bed dating to the 1890s. Another nostalgic escape is the opulent Victorian Suite, with its red-velvet-canopied four-poster bed, crystal chandelier, and elegant sitting room. The plant-filled Garden Suite features trickling fountains and an old-fashioned walnut bed.

A full complimentary breakfast is served on the balcony overlooking Main Street or under the skylight in the lobby. In the afternoon and evening, guests can gather downstairs in the hotel's Western saloon for drinks, billiards, and sing-alongs around the honky-tonk piano.

Located in the heart of downtown—the area known as "Old Bisbee"—the inn is just a few steps away from restaurants, antique shops, art galleries, and a museum.

Bisbee Inn

P.O. Box 1855
45 OK Street
Old Bisbee, Arizona 85603
phone: 520-432-5131

THE BISBEE INN was built in 1916 on the foundation of a building destroyed by a fire that ravaged the hillside. The two-story red-brick structure opened as La More Hotel, a boardinghouse for copper miners. Each of its 24 rooms was often occupied by three miners at a time, each working a different shift. The rooms had wall sinks with hot and cold water, and two commodes and a bathtub were located down the hall. Entertainment waited only a few steps down the hill in rowdy Brewery

Gulch—"the haven of working men's diversions"—which offered 47 saloons and streets lined with "cribs" belonging to ladies of the night. When things got out of hand in Brewery Gulch, offenders were carted up the hill to the city jail.

In the 1940s, the inn was converted into two-room apartments. For a time in the 1960s, the building was leased by the Peace Corps as a training center for volunteers. The structure deteriorated until the early 1980s, when the city finally declared it unfit for habitation. After a period of vacancy, it was purchased by John and Joy Timbers, who with their partner, John Thorup, began the tedious task of restoration.

The plumbing and wiring were replaced, the original woodwork was restored, the metal beds were stripped and repainted, and the wall sinks were repaired and hung in their original locations. Skylights were added to allow filtered light to bathe the Douglas fir staircase and the enclosed atrium, a delightful spot for enjoying the inn's delicious breakfasts. An old-time wooden telephone hangs on the wall near the front door, and interesting black-and-white photos and mining maps decorate the walls throughout.

The guest rooms vary in size, but all are clean and comfortable and are furnished to reflect the hotel's past. Accordingly, there are no telephones or televisions in the rooms, and there is only one color television in the downstairs parlor. Many of the inn's original oak dressers, armoires, and chairs remain in use. And just like the old days, the transoms allow air to circulate. Attractive flowered wallpaper and lace curtains dress up an otherwise simple decor. Four rooms have private baths, and the rest share lavatories and showers, arranged in separate, well-equipped compartments down the hall.

The complimentary breakfast is a bargain not to be taken lightly. In fact, it's a hearty, all-you-can-eat event at which you can stuff yourself silly at one of the lace-covered tables in the cozy breakfast room or in the adjoining sunny courtyard.

Rates

The inn offers 20 rooms. The four rooms with double beds and private baths and the room with a queen-size bed and a shared bath are available for $65. The rooms with double beds and shared baths rent for $50. An all-you-can-eat breakfast is included. Credit cards are not accepted. Children are welcome, but pets are not. Smoking is not allowed. The inn is open all year.

Amenities

A sink is in each room. Some rooms have shared baths and showers. A television is in the parlor and a telephone in the lobby.

Location

The inn is on OK Street near Naco Road.

Calumet & Arizona Guest House

608 Powell Street
Bisbee, Arizona 85603
phone: 520-432-4815
Joy and John Timbers, owners/innkeepers

BACK AT THE TURN OF THE CENTURY, when Bisbee was a booming copper-mining town, mine officials and their families were looking for tranquil sites on which to build their mansions. They envisioned a stable, respectable community in which to live and raise their children, away from Bisbee's bustling streets and rowdy Brewery Gulch. They chose a site about four miles from downtown and named it after a local prospector, George Warren.

Calumet & Arizona Guest House

Today, Warren remains a small, sleepy community tucked around the bend from Bisbee's crowded downtown streets. The elegant old mansions are still there, serving as proud reminders of the town's dignified history. Some have been lovingly restored and converted into bed-and-breakfasts. One of these is the Calumet & Arizona Guest House, an unusual pink-and-white two-story on the corner of Cole and Powell Streets.

The thick-walled adobe structure, designed by noted Southwestern architect Henry Trost, was built in 1906 by the Calumet & Arizona Mining Company for Joseph Curry, the company's chief clerk. Constructed in the Spanish Mission style with a raised medallion above the entrance and intaglio around the porch, the home is truly one of a kind, a standout amid the traditional Midwestern homes lining the neighborhood's streets. Curry, who also served as secretary of the Warren Company and secretary-treasurer of the Apache Powder Company, purchased the home from Calumet & Arizona in 1916 and sold it back to the mining company in 1926. It subsequently became a guesthouse for mining-company VIPs. After Bisbee's mining operations slowed, it was converted into an apartment house and gradually fell into a state of disrepair.

In 1977, the neglected old home was purchased by current owners Joy and John Timbers, who began an ambitious restoration project. For five years, they refinished and embellished the spacious residence. In 1982, they opened on a limited basis to bed-and-breakfast guests. More restoration and expansion followed. In 1992, the entire six-bedroom, 5,000-square-foot home became available to guests.

Prepare to be transported back to another era upon entering this interesting house. High, crowned ceilings, handsome oak and maple floors, wainscoting, distinctive fireplaces, leaded-glass windows, and the original staircase show that the stately residence is still in its prime. The Victorian period is celebrated throughout the entire first floor with handsome antique furnishings and unusual chandeliers. A photo album on a table in the parlor by the copper-paneled fireplace is worth looking through for its before-and-after restoration photos, some dating as far back as 1912.

Three guest rooms are upstairs and three down. All are comfortably and individually furnished. Some have private baths, and others share a bath. The roomy Beige Room upstairs, the most contemporary room in the house, has its own fireplace, sitting area, and bath.

Breakfast, a leisurely, sit-down affair in the elegant downstairs dining room, features delicious homemade items like crepes filled with scrambled eggs and topped with hollandaise sauce. A low, thick wall surrounds the patio and gardens and is a great place to enjoy Bisbee's temperate climate and a last cup of freshly brewed coffee.

Rates

Rooms are available for $45 (single occupancy) to $83 (double occupancy). Children over six months are charged at the full rate. Full breakfast is included. Check-in is from 3 P.M. to 4 P.M. and check-out at 11 A.M. Smoking is not permitted indoors. Well-behaved pets are allowed.

Amenities

Two rooms have private baths and four share baths. The inn offers a courtyard garden, a piano, and afternoon refreshments.

Location

From the traffic circle on AZ 80, exit onto Bisbee Road and follow it into the community of Warren. Turn left on Cole Street and continue to Powell Street. The inn is on the corner on the right. Parking is in front.

Clawson House

Clawson House
P.O. Box 454
116 Clawson Avenue
Old Bisbee, Arizona 85603
phone: 800-467-5237 or 520-432-5237
Jim Grosskopf, innkeeper

PICTURESQUE BISBEE, layered along the steep canyons of the Mule Mountains, reminds some visitors of a miniature, landlocked San Francisco. Perhaps that is why former California residents Wally Kuehl and Jim Grosskopf purchased the handsome structure known as the Clawson House in 1988. After spending two years carefully restoring the structure and furnishing it with their 30-year collection of art and antiques, they opened a bed-and-breakfast.

The regal two-story structure of gray wood trimmed in white was built in 1895 as a single-level residence with a carriage house for Spencer W. Clawson, superintendent of the Copper Queen Mine. The four-acre site the mining executive chose sat high atop Castle Rock overlooking the town. He spared no expense during construction. Many of Clawson's elegant touches remain today, as does a cave under the dining room said to have provided protection from Indian attacks. The original etched Italian windows in the foyer, the crystal chandeliers and built-in china cabinet in the dining room, the elaborate brass hardware, and the gleaming oak floors exist in perfect harmony with the current owners' collectibles. The only change in the building's basic structure occurred in the 1920s, when the second owner, a lawyer named Ellenwood, added the upper floor.

Today's guests have a choice of three well-appointed rooms. The Victorian Room, on the main level, features an impressive mahogany bed with matching vanity, a domed chandelier, and framed Currier and Ives prints. The two upstairs guest rooms are airy and bright and offer excellent views. One has a sitting area and Victorian / Oriental decor; the other has a balcony and is decorated in the Art Deco style of the 1930s. The upstairs rooms share a bath that has a deep claw-foot tub perfect for soaking away the day's cares.

Jim Grosskopf prepares elegant breakfast feasts served with silver and linens and featuring fresh homemade breads warm from the oven, fresh fruit compotes, and tasty Southwestern cheese-and-chile quiches. Although the downstairs breakfast room is cozy, many guests prefer to enjoy the breezes and the views from the glassed-in sunroom or the spacious front porch which runs the length of the house.

Rates

The room with a private bath and the two rooms with a shared bath are available for $65 to $75. Full breakfast is included. Major credit cards are accepted. Small children and pets are not allowed. Smoking is permitted in designated areas only. The inn is open all year.

Amenities

The inn offers cable television, a house phone, overhead fans in the bedrooms, and off-street parking. It is a short walk downhill to Old Bisbee.

Location

Take the business exit off AZ 80 into Old Bisbee. Turn left onto Main Street / Tombstone Canyon Road and continue through town. Began the climb up Castle Rock, watching for Clawson Avenue on the right. After a short, steep climb, Clawson House is the first house on the right.

Copper Queen Hotel

Copper Queen Hotel

11 Howell Street
Drawer CQ
Old Bisbee, Arizona 85603
phone: 800-247-5829 or 520-432-2216
fax: 520-432-4298

AT THE TURN OF THE CENTURY, when Bisbee reigned as the world's largest copper-mining town, it was also known as the best stopover between New Orleans and San Francisco. Mining executives, territorial governors, international dignitaries, and celebrities all traveled to Bisbee to admire the streets lined with stately brick Victorians and other impressive buildings, including two opera houses and the majestic Copper Queen Hotel.

The famous five-story brick hotel was built in 1902 by the Copper Queen Mining Company (later the Phelps Dodge Corporation). Designed in the Italian Villa style by New York architects, it was built at the bottom of the gulch in the heart of downtown Bisbee. From the beginning, the Copper Queen served as a gathering place and social center for distinguished visitors and prominent citizens, while just around the corner at

Brewery Gulch, 40-odd saloons and notorious "shady ladies" provided plenty of entertainment for the miners. The Copper Queen remains a center of activity nearly a century later. With its central location and a guest register that includes such famous names as Teddy Roosevelt, Blackjack Pershing, and John Wayne, "the Queen" is still considered the only place to stay in Bisbee by many.

The glory days of mining operations slowed to a halt by the 1970s, and the town fell into a state of neglect. But unlike other boom towns of the past, Bisbee had sturdy brick structures that endured. Thanks to the foresight of the town's early citizens, Bisbee remains architecturally sound and looks much as it did a century ago. Filmmakers, artists, and photographers enjoy the town's romantic mountainside setting. Many of them check into the recently renovated Queen for a nostalgic trip back to Bisbee in its prime.

The original hotel safe and the old switchboard (finally retired from active service in 1990) still stand in place behind the check-in desk, You'll also see other relics in the lobby area: an old roll-top desk, an antique typewriter, yellowed photos taken during Bisbee's prosperous mining days, and the original creaking staircase leading to the second-floor lobby.

Today, the Queen offers 45 guest rooms, two lobbies, balconies, a heated swimming pool, an award-winning dining room, and an old-time saloon. The long, narrow hallways, which have copper light fixtures and walls lined with interesting old photos, open to high-ceilinged rooms decorated with antique furnishings, lace curtains, and quaint flowered wallpaper. Most of the rooms have been refurbished—but make sure to ask for one. All the rooms have private baths, some with claw-foot tubs. One of the Queen's most asked-for rooms is on the second floor in the corner. It's the one nearest the bar and was once a home away from home for John Wayne.

Friendly ghosts are said to inhabit the colorful Copper Queen Saloon downstairs, offering guests a chance to rub shoulders with some of the governors, gamblers, and celebrities who once stayed and played at the Queen.

High Desert Inn

P.O. Box 145
8 Naco Road
Old Bisbee, Arizona 85603-9998
phone: 800-281-1510 or 520-432-1442
fax: 520-432-1410
Margaret Hartnett and Darrell Lee Dixon, hosts

LIFE WAS GOOD IN BISBEE at the beginning of the 20th century, when copper was plentiful in the mines and whiskey flowed in Brewery Gulch. It was a time when stately city buildings and elegant Victorian residences began to appear on the main streets of the boom town at the base of the Mule Mountains.

Today, downtown Bisbee looks much as it did at the turn of the century, giving visitors a chance to step into the past. The impressive High Desert Inn, a towering, important-looking structure with four columns and a classical facade, demands attention. Built of reinforced concrete around 1910, it originally housed the city jail. Its location—around the corner from the rowdy bars and brothels that once lined the streets of Brewery Gulch—provided a handy base of operations for lawmen. Things quieted down considerably in 1914, when Arizona became a dry state.

A sign at the front door reads, "1918 City Hall and Sheriff Office," thereby announcing another role the structure played in Bisbee's history. Courtrooms and judge's chambers occupied the upper floor, and the jail was located downstairs. With its extra-thick concrete walls and tiny windows, the "tank" was breakout-proof and practically airless. It had a perfect record of no known escapes. Operations at the courthouse and the sheriff's office ceased in 1930, when Bisbee won the county seat from Tombstone and a new Cochise County Courthouse was built up the canyon. Various administrative offices occupied the vacated rooms for a time.

In recent years, the tables have turned. Visitors enjoy escaping to the creatively restored courthouse, which offers modern conveniences, charming guest rooms upstairs, and a gourmet restaurant in the former jail. In 1992, the historic structure was sold at public auction. Renovations began soon afterward. The inn and restaurant opened in March 1994 under the management of trained chef Margaret Hartnett and her partner, Darrell Lee Dixon.

Reminiscent of a cozy European inn, the High Desert Inn has a small, sophisticated lobby with a corner cappuccino/liquor bar where guests can mingle with diners waiting for a table in the dining room, located at the rear of the lobby. The jail door next to the restaurant's entrance and the rusty cell off the patio remind visitors of the building's original purpose.

Five spacious and comfortably furnished guest rooms are located upstairs. Each has deep green carpeting and creamy white walls, queen-size wrought-iron beds from France, handcrafted tables, and a sofa or overstuffed chair. Modern conveniences include private baths, telephones, and color televisions, a rarity in Bisbee accommodations.

Rates

The five rooms are available for $60 to $85. MasterCard, Visa, and Discover are accepted. Breakfast is not included.

Amenities

The rooms have queen-size beds, private baths, color televisions, and telephones. The inn offers a dining room (which serves dinner only on Thursday, Friday, and Saturday), massage therapy, and haircutting and styling.

Location

Take the business exit off AZ 80 into Old Bisbee. Continue under the highway and turn right onto Naco Road. Look for the four-columned High Desert Inn on the left. A parking lot is directly across the street from the inn.

Inn at Castle Rock

P.O. Box 1161
112 Tombstone Canyon Road
Old Bisbee, Arizona 85603
phone: 800-566-4449, 520-432-4449, or 520-432-7195
fax: 520-432-7868
e-mail: theinn@aol.com
Jim and Jeannene Babcock, innkeepers; Bob Etter, operations manager

BISBEE'S BEGINNINGS can be traced to a spring which once bubbled at the base of Castle Rock. It was here, at Apache Spring, that Sergeant Jack Dunn stopped for water in 1877. He noticed traces of silver in the canyon and had claims staked in his name a few months later. Word got around, and before long, other miners were pouring in and digging all over the place. By 1880, the mining camp was ready to be declared the town of Bisbee.

Inn at Castle Rock

When miners dug a shaft too close to the spring at Castle Rock, water broke through, flooding the mine. The spring became the town well for a time and was later abandoned. In 1890, Bisbee's first mayor, a man named Muirhead, built a boardinghouse for miners on the site. The structure was converted into apartments in the 1950s and was opened as a bed-and-breakfast in 1982.

The colorful Inn at Castle Rock—a vibrant red three-story Victorian with cream-colored wraparound balconies—is impossible to ignore even in a town brimming with impressive historic structures. The inn's owner, geologist and artist Jim Babcock, converted the former basement into a warm, sunny restaurant and the old well into a fish pond. The innovative Babcock, who owned an inn in Aspen, Colorado, before moving to Bisbee, solved the problem of a leaking roof by constructing a double **A**-frame loft, which serves as a pleasant upper parlor for guests.

The inn's eclectic interior is as colorful as its exterior. Each of the 15 guest rooms has a different theme, from fussy Victorian to casual South Seas to American Indian. Babcock's artwork is everywhere, and plants tumble from pots. The furnishings are a blend of antiques and vintage 1950s pieces left over from the structure's apartment years. The guest rooms facing the street open out onto balconies that wrap around the front and sides of the building. The rooms at the back have a view of the steep, terraced hillside with its ramadas, trails, and acre of flowers, shrubs, and trees that attract hummingbirds throughout the summer.

The side garden with shaded tables and three fish ponds fascinates children as well as adults.

Breakfast, served from 7:30 to 9:30 every morning, includes fresh baked goods, fruits, cereals, egg dishes, French toast, and other items. At times, guests can enjoy live piano or guitar music with their morning meal at this personable, offbeat, one-of-a-kind inn.

Rates

Rooms are available for $38.50 to $110.00, depending on the number in the party. Credit cards and personal checks are accepted. Breakfast is included. Children and pets are welcome. Smoking is not permitted indoors.

Amenities

The rooms have private baths and twin, full, queen-size, or king-size beds. The inn offers a television in the parlor, a phone, an art gallery, and a restaurant.

Location

Take the business exit off AZ 80 into Old Bisbee. Turn left onto Main Street and follow it as it winds through downtown and becomes Tombstone Canyon Road. The inn is on the left.

Judge Ross House

605 Shattuck Street
Bisbee, Arizona 85603
phone: 520-432-4120 or 520-432-5597
Bonnie and Jim Douglas, hosts

THE JUDGE ROSS HOUSE, a two-story red-brick structure, is located on a quiet street in Warren, a sleepy suburb four miles south of Old Bisbee.

It was constructed in 1908, a year after Warren was connected to Bisbee by a streetcar line, which made commuting quicker and more economical. Perhaps that is the reason Judge Ross of superior court selected a large lot on Shattuck Street on which to build the house that still bears his name.

The handsome structure which once housed the judge and his extensive law library was bought and sold a few times before longtime Bisbee-area residents Jim and Bonnie Douglas purchased it in the late 1970s. The judge's library was shipped off to the county courthouse, and the Douglases spent two years renovating the interior of the 3,000-square-foot home. In 1982, with their 45-year collection of exquisite antiques in place, they opened the historic home as a bed-and-breakfast.

Guests have the run of the upper level, which includes two bedrooms (each with a private bath), a sunny, glass-enclosed porch, and a living room with a vaulted ceiling, well-stocked bookshelves, a television, and a VCR. The guest rooms reflect the romantic Victorian theme. Among their features are delicate floral wallpaper, quilts, a towel steamer from an old barber shop, and a brass bed said to have belonged to a notorious madam from El Paso.

Fresh flowers and candy-filled dishes add a welcoming touch throughout the gracious house, which is also the setting for Bonnie Douglas's popular formal tea parties. Outside, terraced gardens and a tree-shaded patio are perfect for relaxing and nibbling on Bonnie's scrumptious home-made breakfast, although the formal dining room and the upstairs sun porch are fine alternatives.

Rates

The two rooms are available for $60 (single occupancy) or $65 (double occupancy). Full breakfast is included. Small children and pets are not allowed. Visa and MasterCard are accepted.

Main Street Inn

P.O. Box 454
26 Main Street
Old Bisbee, Arizona 85603
phone: 800-467-5237 or 602-432-5237
Wally Kuehl, innkeeper

THE STATELY HISTORIC STRUCTURES lining Main Street today look much the same as they did a century ago, when Bisbee was in its prime. The buildings reflect the importance of the formerly copper-rich town, once one of the most powerful communities in the state.

The structure which houses the Main Street Inn was built in 1888 as the Mann Hotel and is the only building on the street with bay windows. The inn actually occupies the second level of two buildings joined above a ground floor that once housed the original Goldwater's Department Store. Today, a natural-food store and a combination tobacco shop and pool room are located below the inn.

After its years as a boardinghouse for copper miners, the building was converted into county offices and shops. Then partners Wally Kuehl and Jim Grosskopf, who own the Clawson House up the hill, purchased the Main Street structure. After restoration was completed in 1992, they

Main Street Inn

opened the Main Street Inn. Every morning since then, Jim has prepared a continental breakfast at the Clawson House and Wally has delivered it, warm from the oven, to his guests at the Main Street Inn.

A narrow stairway leads from the Main Street entrance to the elaborately furnished inn. Eight inviting guest rooms and a three-room corner suite are tastefully furnished in the Southwestern style with handcrafted solid-oak pieces made in nearby Sierra Vista. Thick carpeting provides a good sound barrier against noises below, and the 12-foot ceilings and original skylights lend a feeling of space. Other things from the old days remain: a claw-foot tub, brick walls, and closets. The popular Honeymoon Suite features a large skylight and a mirrored wall, leftovers from the room's previous role as a beauty shop.

Guests may also use the inn's back entrance, located at the top of the stairway on Commerce Street. This entrance opens into a comfortable porch that stretches across the back of the building. The inn's "quiet room" and separate television lounge provide a convenient and cozy respite from Main Street, which can really draw crowds on weekends.

The inn's location in the center of the historic district puts guests within easy walking distance of the shops, art galleries, and restaurants in the town's turn-of-the-century buildings. A favorite destination for photographers and history buffs, Bisbee is also popular with filmmakers, who like the town's ability to double as a European mountain village.

Rates

The eight rooms are available for $45 to $95. Continental breakfast is included. Personal checks, Visa, and MasterCard are accepted. Pets are not allowed. Smoking is restricted to designated areas.

Amenities

Three rooms share two baths; four other rooms share two baths; and the two-bedroom suite has a private bath. The inn offers a house phone, off-street parking, a quiet room, and a television room.

Location

Take the business exit off AZ 80 into Old Bisbee. Turn left onto Main Street. The inn is on the left in the second block.

OK Street Jailhouse

P.O. Box 1152
9 OK Street
Old Bisbee, Arizona 85603
phone: 800-821-0678 or 520-432-7435
fax: 520-432-7434
Doris Turner, manager

INMATES AT THE OK STREET JAILHOUSE during the early 1900s never had it as good as those who "do time" here today. Behind the same barred windows and thick concrete walls, present-day inmates serve self-imposed sentences in a fancy 1,200-square-foot suite.

The narrow two-story structure on OK Street was built in 1904 as the local branch of the Cochise County Jail. It sits a block away from notori-

OK Street Jailhouse

ous Brewery Gulch, where rowdy bars catered to miners and beer flowed in the streets. By 1915, the small jail was unable to handle the crush of prisoners during Bisbee's mining boom and was closed when a larger facility was built. For decades, the jailhouse on OK Street remained empty. Finally, in 1988, it was renovated into a comfortable two-level suite.

The former jailer's office, off the tiled entry downstairs, now serves as a small sitting room with a desk, a phone, and a life-size cardboard cut-out of John Wayne in cowboy attire. The tribute to the Duke stems from Wayne's part-ownership of the jailhouse during the 1950s, when Bisbee was a popular Western movie site.

The old drunk tank, where iron bars stretch from floor to ceiling, has been cleverly remodeled and now holds a contemporary living room with a sofa bed, an Indian print rug, and old photos of Bisbee's heyday. A few steps away are a half-bath and a small kitchen with a serving counter and barstools.

The bedroom suite is located upstairs in the cell that once held the jail's serious offenders. The heavy bars are still there, but today's accommodations are plush. There's a cozy sitting area overlooking the street, a bedroom with a queen-size bed, and a modern bathroom with a Mexican-tile floor and a mirror above the Jacuzzi.

Guests lucky enough to arrange a sentence at the jailhouse have the entire building to themselves, which makes it a favorite with honeymooners and families. Parking is just a few steps from the front door, but you probably won't have much use for a car. Bisbee's streets are lined with well-preserved historic buildings housing an assortment of shops and fine restaurants, all within walking distance of the jail.

Rates

The two-story suite is available for $100 for one night and $75 for each additional night; the rate for a week's stay is $450. Visa and MasterCard are accepted. Pets are allowed by prearrangement.

Amenities

The suite has a kitchenette with a serving counter, one and a half baths, a Jacuzzi, two sitting rooms, a television in the living room, a queen-size bed, a queen-size sofa bed, a telephone, and off-street parking in a public lot. It is convenient to downtown Bisbee.

Location

The jailhouse is on OK Street off Naco Road in downtown Bisbee.

Oliver House

24 Sowle Avenue
Old Bisbee, Arizona 85603
phone: 520-432-4286
Dennis Schranz, owner/innkeeper

A FOOTBRIDGE stretching over a canal leads the way to the Oliver House, a two-story red-brick structure with a hip roof. Perched on a slope above Main Street in downtown Bisbee, the building was erected in 1909 to house mining executives. The owner, Edith Ann Oliver, named the building for her husband, Henry, who amassed a fortune in mining.

Ghost stories abound at the Oliver House, most of them stemming from the 1920s, when shootings occurred in the building. One shooting remains unsolved, and another was the result of a love triangle gone wrong. One of the best stories involves current owner Dennis Schranz, who, when purchasing the neglected structure in 1986, ignored the former owner's claim that five ghosts—one of them violent—inhabited the house. During his first night as owner, the skeptical Schranz heard strange sounds in the building and witnessed his puppy's refusal to enter the house. He summoned a Catholic priest, who blessed everything in the house. The cleansing seems to have quieted the ghosts, but not the stories.

The character of the former boardinghouse remains today at the inn, which does not cater to those seeking luxurious accommodations. The rooms are unpretentious, clean, and reasonably priced. They have sparse furnishings, original pine floors, high ceilings, and leaded-glass windows. Rooms on the main level share bathrooms, while those upstairs have private baths. The views from some of the second-story bedrooms sweep across downtown Bisbee and Main Street at the bottom of the gulch, a short walk down the hill from the inn. Forget television and radio, because entertainment here is like it was in the early days: books, games, and friendly conversation in the cozy living room, which doubles as a dining room when breakfast is set out in the morning.

Rates

The 12 rooms (some with private baths, some with shared baths) are available for $43.50 to $84.50. Breakfast is included. Major credit cards are accepted. No pets are allowed.

Amenities

The inn offers a living room, a dining room, and a phone. It is convenient to downtown attractions.

School House Inn

School House Inn

P.O. Box 32
818 Tombstone Canyon
Bisbee, Arizona 85603
phone/fax: 800-537-4333 or 520-432-2996
Jeff and Bobby Blankenbeckler, owners/innkeepers

BISBEE WAS REBORN IN THE 1970S, when many of the old mining town's stately and sturdy historic structures were remodeled into charming accommodations, not two of which are alike.

Take the School House Inn on Bisbee's west side in the Tombstone Canyon neighborhood. As its name implies, the inn was once a school, the former two-story Garfield Primary School. Built in 1918, it was constructed with no-nonsense masonry walls, high ceilings, and wide stairways. The school's blueprints, on display in the main stairway near the principal's office, show the four large classrooms for grades 1 through 4.

Like most of the town's historic buildings, the school survived by being adapted to new roles. During the 1930s, the classrooms were converted into apartments. In the 1970s, the building became a nursing home. In 1989, it was transformed into a charming bed-and-breakfast. Seven years later, it was sold to current owners Jeff and Bobby Blankenbeckler.

Great efforts have been made to preserve the memory of the inn's former educational role, as guests will see when they check in at the desk used by the school's first principal. The old class photos lining the stairway wall were donated by old-timers who remember attending school in the building. You can bet the old schoolrooms were never so appealing as they are today. The spacious guest rooms have 12-foot ceilings, comfortable country-style furnishings, and private baths. Each room's decor reflects a particular subject. The Geography Room has a collection of maps, for example, and the History Room has shelves lined with Arizona history books and a cozy reading nook. The institutional feeling of the building has been softened by the owners' homey touches: area rugs over the original maple floors and lace curtains at the windows. School days were never so enjoyable.

Stunning views of upper Tombstone Canyon and the Mule Mountains add to the inn's appeal. And as you might expect at a former school, there's an adjacent park with a court for basketball and volleyball and a playground. Off-street parking is right outside the door.

Because Bisbee's mile-high climate protects it from summer heat and winter cold, the side patio under a sprawling oak tree is a favorite year-round retreat. Guests claim that the patio, where a fountain bubbles and hummingbirds dart among the many feeders, is the perfect setting for the inn's hearty home-style breakfasts and steaming cups of freshly ground coffee.

Rates

The six guest rooms and three two-bedroom suites are available for $50 to $70. Breakfast is included. Children over 14 are welcome. Major credit cards are accepted. Pets are not permitted. No smoking is allowed indoors.

Douglas

Gadsden Hotel

Gadsden Hotel

1046 G Avenue
Douglas, Arizona 85607
phone: 520-364-4481
Robin Brekhus, resident manager

NO ARIZONA STRUCTURE epitomizes the glamour of the Old West better than the Gadsden Hotel. The one-time grande dame may be showing her age today, but the magnificent lobby—with its vaulted stained-glass skylights, its curving white-marble staircase, and its soaring marble columns topped in 14-carat gold leaf—reflects the opulence of the period like no other.

Located a mile from the Mexican border, the splendid Gadsden Hotel has been a center of activity in Douglas since its opening in 1907. Scores of dignitaries and celebrities including Eleanor Roosevelt, Charles Lindbergh, Amelia Earhart, Alan Ladd, Paul Newman, and every governor of Arizona have stayed at the Gadsden. Thanks to its glamorous past and Old World grandeur, the Gadsden continues to attract filmmakers, who have featured the hotel in numerous movies.

Today, ghost stories and legends keep the past alive at this "last of the grand hotels," where in 1912 famous Mexican desperado Pancho Villa reportedly rode his horse up the lobby's staircase, leaving a nasty nick in his wake. Some say the renegade's headless, caped ghost returns occasionally to haunt the hallways.

The massive five-story structure was designed by celebrated Southwestern architect Henry Trost. It was named after the Gadsden Purchase of 1853, which granted the Mexican territory south of the Gila River to the United States. Although a fire demolished most of the original building in 1927, a new hotel was constructed a year later on the foundation of the first. The same Trost design was used for the new hotel, except for two changes: structural steel and reinforced concrete replaced the brick-and-frame construction of the original, and the main entrance was moved to G Avenue. No cost was spared during construction. The Gadsden featured the finest materials and fixtures, including a copper plumbing system.

Named a National Historic Site in 1976, the hotel fell into disrepair a decade later. Rescue came when Hartman and Doris Brekhus, wheat farmers from North Dakota who remembered many enjoyable winter visits at the old hotel, purchased the Gadsden in 1988. With the aid and energy of their daughter-in-law, Robin, the resident manager, Hartman and Doris set out to return the old hotel to its former glory. Since the Gadsden has 160 guest rooms, a restaurant, shops, a saloon, and innumerable fancy fixtures, restoration is an ongoing affair. But room by room, floor by floor, the monumental task is being done, and the effect is proving to be worth the wait.

The second floor is a good place for browsing, especially if you climb the wide marble stairs. You'll be rewarded with fine views of the downstairs lobby and the stained-glass mural above the staircase. You'll also be able to inspect the ornate gold-leaf pillars and browse through the interesting collection of old photos, historical documents, and other artifacts on display.

The guest rooms vary in size and are decorated as they appear in old photos taken in the 1920s and 1930s. Unlike the ornate lobby, most of the rooms are uncluttered. They feature early Southwestern and Mexican decor, with handsome chests and tables inlaid with colorful hand-painted tiles.

Rates
The 160 rooms with private baths rent for $32 to $85. Suites and apartments with kitchenettes are also available. Credit cards are accepted. Pets are not allowed.

Amenities
The rooms have telephones and televisions. The hotel offers a restaurant, a saloon, a beauty shop, and a large lobby.

Location
The hotel is in downtown Douglas at the corner of G Avenue and 11th Street.

Adobe Rose Inn Bed-and-Breakfast, 139–41

Agua Fria River, 42, 93

Agua Prieta, 121

Ajo lodgings, 135–39

Alpine lodgings and attractions, 42, 85–87

Amado lodgings, 192–94

Anasazi Indians, xv, 4, 12

Angel and the Badman, 38

Apache Lumber Company, 74

Apache Mountains, 41

Apache Powder Company, 214

Apache Spring, 222

Arizona, xvii

Arizona Biltmore, xvii, 43, 101–3

Arizona Inn, 141–43

Arizona State Museum, 140

Arizona Territory, 41, 114, 192

Arizona–Sonoran Desert Museum, 121

Astaire, Fred, 115

Baboquivari, 204

Banters, Jennie, 46

Barrio Elysian Grove, 153

Barrows Boarding House, 189

Batterton, Harry, 168

Beaver Creek, 44

Benton, Arthur, 114

Berlin, Irving, 102

Best Western Coronado Motor Hotel, 132–34

Big Nose Kate's Saloon, 188

Birch Tree Inn, xviii, 19–21

Bird Cage Theater, 188

Bisbee Grand Hotel, 209–11

Bisbee Inn, 211–13

Bisbee lodgings and attractions, xvi, xvii, 120, 209–34

Black Stallion, The, 176

Blixen, Karen, 161

Blue Range Primitive Area, 86

Bogart, Humphrey, xvii, 23–24, 25

Boudreaux, L. J., 148

Boys on the Side, 154

Bradshaw Mountains, 89

Brewery Gulch, 211–12, 213, 219, 221

Briar Patch Inn, 28–30

Bright Angel Camp, 8

Bright Angel Hotel, 7–8

Bright Angel Lodge, 7–9, 16

Broken Arrow, 38, 200

Broken Lance, 200

Buffalo Bill, 130

Buford, George, 185

Buford House, 184–86

Bureau of Land Management, 181, 207

Butler, John T., 78

Butler, Molly, 78–79

Byers, Abby, 59

Call of the Canyon, 38

Calumet & Arizona Guest House, 213–15

Calumet & Arizona Mining Company, 214

Camelback Inn. *See* Marriott's

Camelback Inn
Camelback Mountain, 97, 106, 108
Camp Verde, 44
Canyon de Chelly National Monument, xvi, 4, 5, 12, 13
Canyon del Muerto, 5
Carlson, Arthur, 52
Carlson, Maude, 52
Carrillo, Emilio, 170
Carrillo, Leopoldo, 153
Carrillo's Garden, 153
Carson, Johnny, 96
Casa Alegre Bed-and-Breakfast Inn, 144–45
Casa de Coronado, 132
Casa Hermosa, 99, 100
Casablanca, 25
Cassidy, Hopalong, xvii, 38
Castle Rock, 216, 222, 223
Catalina Park, 146
Catalina Park Inn, 146–48
Chandler, A. J., 114, 115
Chandler lodgings and attractions, xvii, 43, 114–16
Chapel of the Holy Cross (Sedona), 5–6
Chinle lodgings and attractions, 5, 12–14
Chiricahua Apache, 119
Circle Z Ranch, 199–201
Clanton, Billy, 189
Clark, Elias S., 26
Clawson House, 216–17, 226
Clawson, Spencer W., 216
Cleopatra Hill, 41
Clinkscale, J. H., 47
Cochise, 119

Cochise County Courthouse, 190, 221
Cochise County Jail, 221, 228
Coconino National Forest, 20
Colbert, Claudette, 161
Coldstream Bed-and-Breakfast, The, 73–75
Colorado River, 3, 5, 11, 22, 78, 120
Colter, Mary Jane, 5, 8, 9
Converse, Jim, 171
Cooke, Delos, 106–7
Cooke, Florence, 106–7
Cooper, Gary, 23
Copper Bell Bed-and-Breakfast, 148–50
Copper Queen Hotel, xvi, xvii, 218–20
Copper Queen Mine, 216
Copper Queen Mining Company, 218
Copper Queen Saloon, 219
Coronado, Francisco Vasquez de, 85
Coronado Motor Hotel. See Best Western Coronado Motor Hotel
Coronado Trail, 85
Cotten, Joseph, 162
Cottonwood, 52
Courthouse Plaza (Prescott), xvi, 42, 55, 58, 60, 61, 62, 63, 67, 71
Coyote's Grill and Cantina, 77
Crawford, Joan, 115
Crystal Palace, 188
Cuban Queen, the, 46
Curley, Michael, 137
Curry, Joseph, 214

Davis, Bette, 96

Day, Sam, 13
De Grazia Gallery in the Sun, 121
De Grazia, Ted, 121
DeNiza, Marcos, 114
Desert Botanical Garden, 44
Desert Caballeros Western Museum, 92
Dierker House Bed-and-Breakfast, 21–23
Dillinger, John, 158, 168
Douglas lodgings and attractions, xvii, 121, 234–36
Douglas, William O., 205
Drachman, Emanuel, 153
Dragoon lodgings, 182–84
Dragoon Mountains, 182
Duke, John, 57
Duke, Mamie, 57
Duncan, Isadora, 161
Dunn, Jack, 222
Duquesne House Bed-and-Breakfast, The, 202–4
Duquesne Mine, 203

Eagar lodgings, 83–85
Earhart, Amelia, 235
Earp, Wyatt, xvi, 57
Eisenhower, Dwight D., 96, 205
Eisenhower, Mamie, 96
"El Hoyo." See Barrio Elysian Grove
El Presidio Bed-and-Breakfast Inn, 150–52
El Presidio District, 121
El Tovar Hotel, 5, 9–12
Elysian Grove, 153
Elysian Grove Market Bed-and-Breakfast Inn, 153–55
Eureka Ranch, 178

Faye, Alice, 133
Fendig, Fred, 200
Ferber, Edna, 102
Flagstaff Community Hotel, 24
Flagstaff lodgings and attractions, xvii, 4, 7, 19–28
Florence lodgings, 123–26
Ford, Henry, III, 113
Forest Houses, 31–33
Fort Huachuca, 189
Fort Lowell, 170
Fred Harvey Company, 5, 8, 9, 10

Gable, Clark, xvii, 102, 110, 155
Gadsden Hotel, xvii, 121, 234–36
Gadsden Purchase, 119, 192, 202, 205, 235
Galiuro Mountains, 179
Garfield Primary School, 232–33
Garland's Oak Creek Lodge, 33–35
Geronimo, 119
Ghost City Inn Bed-and-Breakfast, 45–46
Gila River, 119, 235
Gila River Valley, 128
Globe lodgings and attractions, 41, 116–18
Goldberg, Whoopi, 154
Goldfield Mountains, 112
Goldwater, Barry, 39
Goldwater's Department Store, 226
Goodyear Tire and Rubber Company, 42, 93
Governor's Mansion (Prescott), 43
Grace H. Flandrau Science Center and Planetarium, 141
Graham County, 128
Grand Canyon lodgings and

attractions, xvi, 3, 5, 7–12, 15, 16, 18, 26
Grand Canyon Railway, 3, 8, 15, 18
Grand Canyon Village, 3, 5, 8
Greenway, Isabella, 142, 143
Greenway, John, 138
Greer Lakes, 42
Greer lodgings and attractions, xviii, 42, 78–82
Greer Valley, 80
Grey, Zane, xvii, 24, 38, 79
Guest House Inn, The, 134–36

Hacienda del Sol Guest Ranch Resort, 155–57
Hacienda Los Encinos, 198
Hamaker, Rex, 193
Hannagan Meadow Lodge, 85–87
Harvey, Fred, 8
Harvey Girls, 8, 11
Hassayampa Inn, xvii, 54–56
Hassayampa River, 89
Hayden, Carl, 114
Heard Museum, 44
Hepburn, Katharine, 155
Hereford Dairy Farm, 207
Hereford lodgings, 207–8
Heritage Square, 44
Hermosa Inn, 98–100, 107, 113
Herndon, John C., 71, 72
High Chaparral, 176
High Desert Inn, xvii, 220–22
Hohokam Indians, xv, 43
Holbert, Edith, 146
Holbert, Harry E., 146
Holliday, Doc, xvi
Hon-Dah Casino, 75

Hooker, Henry Clay, 180
Hooker's Hot Springs, 180
Hoover, Herbert, 115
Hopi House, 4
Hopi Indian Reservation, 4
Hotel Burke, 56
Hotel Congress, xvi, 157–59
Hotel Monte Vista, xvii, 23–25
Hotel San Marcos, 114
Hotel St. Michael, 56–58
Hotel Vendome, 59–61
Howard, Jess, 33
Hughes, Sam, 139

Inn at Castle Rock, 222–24
Inn at 410 Bed-and-Breakfast, 26–28
Inn at Jerome, 47–48
Inn at Rancho Sonora, 123–24
Isaacson, Demming, 180

Jaastad, Henry O., 148
James, Harry, 110
Jenkins, Dick, 205
Jerome Grand Hotel, 49–51
Jerome lodgings and attractions, 41, 45–53
Joesler, Josias T., 155, 160
Johnstonian Bed-and-Breakfast, The, 15–18
Judge Ross House, 224–26

Kaull, L. P., 52
Kay El Bar Guest Ranch, 88–90
Kennedy, John F., 182
King, Glendy, 179–80
Kino, Eusebio, 120, 122, 196
Kissinger, Dottie, 112, 113

Kissinger, Henry, 102

Kittridge, Mary, 32

Kittridge, Robert, 31–32

Knibbie, W., 193

Kruttschnitt, Julius, 151

La More Hotel, 211

La Posada del Valle, 160–62

Ladd, Alan, 24, 235

Ladd, William, 130

Lakeside lodgings and attractions,
    42, 76–77

Lakeview Lodge, 76–77

"Last Cattle Drive, The," 183

Lazy K Bar Guest Ranch, 162–65

Leslie, Buckskin Frank, 189

LeSueur, Elna, 83

LeSueur, William F., 83

Life and Times of Judge Roy Bean, The,
    xvii

Lincoln, Abraham, 119

Lincoln, John C., 96, 97

Lindbergh, Charles, 235

Lininger, Cornelia, 166

Lininger, Homer, 166

Lininger, Schuyler W., 166

Linkletter, Art, 177

Litchfield lodgings and attractions,
    42, 93–95

Litchfield, Paul, 42, 93

Little Colorado River, 42, 78, 80

Little Daisy Mine, 48

Lodge on the Desert, The, 165–67

Lomacasi Cottages Bed-and-Break-
    fast, 36–38

Lombard, Carole, 23, 110

Lookout Studio, 5

Los Abrigados Resort and Spa, 37

Lost Dutchman Mine, 113

Lowden, Frank O., 115

Lowdermilk, Romaine, 88

Luke Air Force Base, 94

Lund, Agnes, 80

Lund, Marion, 80

Lund, William, 80

Main Street Inn, 226–28

Maitland, Beth, 62

Mann Hotel, 226

Maricopa Manor Bed-and-Breakfast
    Inn, 103–5

Marks House Cookbook, The, 63

Marks House, The, 61–63

Marks, Jake, 61–62

Marks, Josephine, 62

Marriott, J. W., Sr., xvii, 96

Marriott's Camelback Inn, xvii, 43,
    96–98

Marshall, Thomas, 114–15

Martin, Mary, 113

Martinez, Jesus, 125

Marvin, Lee, 200

Marx, Groucho, 107

Marx, Harpo, 102

Mayo, Virginia, 177

McEntire, Reba, 96

McGuireville, 4

McMurray, Jessica, 180

McNary, 73

McSparron, Leon "Cozy," 13

Megargee, Alonzo "Lon," 98–99,
    100, 113

Mesa lodgings and attractions, 43,
    111–14

MetropolitanTucson Convention and
    Visitors Bureau, 121
Miller, Howard, 178
Mine Manager's House Inn, The,
    137–39
Mingus Mountain, 49, 52
Mission San Jose de Tumacacori, 122
Mission San Xavier del Bac, 120, 121
Mitchell, Margaret, 205
Mix, Tom, xvii, 55, 57, 123, 133
Mofford, Rose, 117
Molly Butler Lodge, xviii, 78–80
Monroe, Marilyn, 102
Monte Walsh, 200
Montezuma Castle National Monu-
    ment, 44
Montosa Ranch, 193
Morenci, 85
Morton, Emily, 190–91
Mount Vernon Inn, 63–65
Mule Mountains, 120, 209, 216,
    220, 233
Mule Pass Gulch, 209
Muleshoe Ranch, 179–81
Mummy Mountain, 97
Murphy, Audie, 162

Nash, Mrs. Preston, 200
Nash, Preston, 200
Nason, Beverly, 173
Nason, Bob, 173
National Park Service Visitor Center
    (Grand Canyon Village), 4
Nature Conservancy, 180, 181
Navajo Indian Reservation, 12
Navajo Indians, 12, 13
Negri, Pola, 161

New Cornelia Copper Company,
    135, 137
New Mexico Territory, 119
Newman, Paul, 235
Noftsger, A., 117
Noftsger Hill Inn, 116–18
Noftsger Hill School, 117
North Globe Schoolhouse, 117
Northern Arizona University, 20, 27

Oak Creek, 6, 31, 33, 36
Oak Creek Canyon, 4, 6, 29, 31, 32,
    33, 38
OK Corral, xvi, 120, 185, 186, 188
OK Street Jailhouse, xvi, 228–30
Old Bisbee, 120, 210
Old Dominion Mine, 118
Old Pueblo Trolley, 168
Old Town Scottsdale, 44
Old Tucson Film Studios, xvii, 122
Oliver, Edith Ann, 231
Oliver, Henry, 231
Oliver House, 230–32
Olney, George A., 127
Olney House Bed-and-Breakfast,
    127–29
Oracle lodgings, 129–31
Oraibi, 4
Overland Route, 120

Painted Desert, 5
Paisley Corner Bed-and-Breakfast,
    83–85
Papago Indians, 134, 204
Papago Park, 44
Paradise Valley lodgings, 98–100
Patagonia lodgings and attractions,

120, 199–204
Patagonia Mountains, 202, 203
Patagonia–Sonoita Creek Preserve,
    203
Peach, John, 132
Peach, Marie, 132
Peacock Dining Room, 55
Pearl, Madam, 46
Penney, J. C., 96
Peppertrees Bed-and-Breakfast Inn,
    167–69
Pershing, John "Blackjack," 182, 219
Phelps Dodge Corporation, 135,
    209, 218
Phelps Dodge Guest House, 135
Phelps Dodge Mining Company, 50
Phoenix lodgings and attractions,
    xvii, 43, 101–10
Pima County Courthouse, 121
Pinal Mountains, 118
Pinetop Country Club, 74
Pinetop lodgings and attractions, 42,
    73–75
Pleasant Street Inn Bed-and-Break-
    fast, 66–68
Pollock, Thomas, 27
Prescott lodgings and attractions,
    xvi, 41, 42, 54–73
Prescott National Forest, 68
Prescott Pines Inn, 68–70
Prescott Police Department, 66
Priscilla's Bed-and-Breakfast, 186–88
Purtyman, Jess, 36

Quarty, John, 115

Rancho de la Osa, 204–6

Rancho Soledad, 124
Rancho Sonora RV Park, 123
Reagan, Nancy, 102
Reagan, Ronald, 102
Recipes from Peppertrees, 169
Red Garter Bed-and-Bakery, 17–18
Revenge of the Nerds, 146
Rex Ranch, 192–94
Richardson, Rollin, 202
Rincon Mountains, 170
Riordan State Historic Park, 5
Robinson, John H., 64
Rockwell, Norman, 113
Rogers, Will, 57
Roosevelt Dam, 43
Roosevelt, Eleanor, 142, 235
Roosevelt, Franklin, 182
Roosevelt, Theodore "Teddy," 23, 57,
    142, 219
Rosson House, 44
Route 66, 24
Royal Palms, 43, 106–8
Rubenstein, Helena, 107
Russell, Jane, xvii, 23

Saddle Rock Ranch, xvii, 38–40
Safford lodgings, 127–29
Saguaro Lake, 111
Saguaro Lake Ranch Resort, 111–14
Salt River, 43, 111, 112, 113
Salt River Project, 43
San Carlos Hotel, xvi, 43, 109–11
San Francisco Peaks, 4, 20, 36, 49
San Marcos Resort, xvii, 43, 114–16
San Pedro Riparian National
    Conservation Area, 207

San Pedro River, 207
San Pedro River Inn, 207–8
San Xavier del Bac Mission. *See* Mission San Xavier del Bac
Sanger, Margaret, 115
Santa Catalina Mountains, xvii, xviii, 129, 130, 155, 161, 166, 172, 174
Santa Cruz River, 195
Santa Cruz Valley, 120, 163
Santa Fe Railroad, 10
Santa Rita Mountains, 199, 202
Sasabe lodgings, 204–6
School House Inn, 232–34
Scott, Randolph, xvii, 38
Scottsdale lodgings and attractions, xvii, 43, 44, 96–98
Sedona lodgings and attractions, xvii, 4, 28–40, 46, 49
Sentinel Peak, 148
Seven Cities of Cibola, 10, 85
Sharlot Hall Museum, 43
Sheraton San Marcos,115
Showers, Byron, 103
Showers, Naomi, 103
Shula, Don, 96
Sierrita Mountains, 204
Silver, Leon, 183
Sinagua Indians, 44
Smith, Harvey, 91
Sombrero Ranch Bed-and-Breakfast, 91–93
Sonoita lodgings and attractions, 120, 197–99
Sonoran Desert, 119
Southern Pacific Railroad, 158
Spencer, William Sturgus, 205

Squaw Peak, 101
St. Michael's Alley, 58
St. Paul's Episcopal Church (Tombstone), 187
Staggs, Elmer A., 163
Stanwyck, Barbara, 24
Starkweather, M. J., 172
Staude, Marguerite, 5
Stevenson, Adlai, 205
Stewart, Jack, 96
Stewart, Jimmy, xvii, 38, 96, 177
Stewart Mountain Dam, 112
Stovall, Al, 106
Sun Yat-sen, 57
Sunrise Park Resort, 42, 75
Sunstone Hotel Investors, 115
Superstition Mountains, 112, 113
Surgeon's House Bed-and-Breakfast, The, 51–53
Swanson, Gloria, 115
Swilling, Jack, 43

Tanque Verde Ranch, xviii, 170–72
Tap Room (Hotel Congress), 158
Taylor's Bed-and-Breakfast, 125–26
Tetzlaff, August, 17
Texas Canyon, 182
Texas Trail, The, 38
Thumb Butte, 62, 65
Thunderbird Lodge, 12–14
Thurber, J. Wilbur, 7
Tlaquepaque, 6
Todd, Bill, 34
Todd, Catherine, 34
Todd, Frank, 34
Tohono O'Odham Reservation, 120, 122, 148

Tom Mix Monument, 123

Tombstone Boarding House Bed-and-
Breakfast Inn, 188–90

Tombstone Canyon, 232, 233

Tombstone lodgings and attractions,
xvi, 120, 184–92

Tonto National Forest, 111

Tovar, Don Pedro de, 10

Towne, Brew, 175–76

Towne, Marge, 175–76

Tracy, Spencer, 155, 200

Travis, W. E., 106

Triangle L Ranch, 129–31

Triangle T Guest Ranch, 182–84

Trost, Henry, 55, 214, 235

Trowbridge, William, 130

Trujillo, Jose, 153–54

Tubac lodgings and attractions, 122,
195–97

Tucker, Sophie, 161

Tucson lodgings and attractions, xvii,
xviii, 119–20, 139–79

Tucson Mountain Park, 121

Tucson Mountains, 162, 175, 177

Tumacacori lodgings, 195–97

Tumacacori National Historical Park,
122, 196

Tutt, Catherine, 182

Tutt, M. J., 130

United States Forest Service, 181

United Verde Copper Company, 49,
52

United Verde Hospital, 49

University of Arizona, 120, 139,
140, 143, 145, 148, 161, 168

University of Arizona Medical
Center, 142, 160–61

Valle Verde Ranch Bed-and-Breakfast,
195–97

Valley National Bank, 128

"Valley of the Sun, the," 43

Verde Valley, 46, 48, 49, 52, 53

Victorian Inn of Prescott, 71–73

Victoria's Bed-and-Breakfast, 190–92

Villa, Pancho, 121, 235

Vineyard Bed-and-Breakfast, The,
197–99

Vulture Mine, 42, 91

Vulture Peak, 91

Wagner, Robert, 162

Waldhouse, Joseph, 20

Walker, Nora Rose, 37

Warren, 213–14, 225

Warren Company, 214

Warren, George, 213

Washington, George, 23

Watchtower, the, 5

Watson, Mary, 172–73

Watson, William, 172–73

Wayne, John, xvii, 38, 177, 219, 229

Webb, Del, 110

Wenck, H. E., 189

Westward Look Resort, xvii–xviii,
172–74

Whiskey Row, 56–57, 60

White Mountain Apache, 42, 74

White Mountain Lodge, 80–82

White Mountains lodgings and
attractions, 42, 73–87

White Stallion Guest Ranch, 175–77

Whittlesley, Charles, 5, 10

Wickenburg, Henry, 42, 91

Wickenburg lodgings and attractions, xviii, 42, 88–92

Wigwam Resort, The, 42, 93–95
Wild Horse Ranch Resort, 177–79
Willcox lodgings, 179–81
Williams lodgings and attractions, 3,
    15–18
Wilson, J. A., 26
Winfrey, Oprah, 96
Wright, Frank Lloyd, xvii, 5, 101,
    102
Wrigley, William, Jr., xvii, 101

Yavapai County Courthouse, 42
Young and the Restless, The, 62
Yuma Crossing, 120
Yuma Landing Restaurant and
    Lounge, 133
Yuma lodgings and attractions, 120,
    132–34

Zimmerman, Max, 175